S0-AJJ-218

Photo by Steve Schapiro

HARRY ANDERSON'S
GAMES YOU CAN'T LOSE
A GUIDE FOR SUCKERS

by Harry Anderson
and Turk Pipkin

POCKET BOOKS

New York   London   Toronto   Sydney   Tokyo

Every effort has been made to trace the copyright holders of the photos used in this volume. Should there be any omissions in this respect, the publisher apologizes and shall be pleased to make the appropriate acknowledgments in any future printings.

An *Original* Publication of POCKET BOOKS

POCKET BOOKS, a division of Simon & Schuster Inc.
1230 Avenue of the Americas, New York, NY 10020

Copyright © 1989 by Harry Anderson and Turk Pipkin

Cover photo by Steve Schapiro
Illustrations by Charlie Snyder

All rights reserved, including the right to reproduce
this book or portions thereof in any form whatsoever.
For information address Pocket Books, 1230 Avenue
of the Americas, New York, NY 10020

ISBN: 0-671-64727-X

First Pocket Books trade paperback printing April 1989

10 9 8 7 6 5 4 3 2 1

POCKET and colophon are trademarks
of Simon & Schuster Inc.

Printed in the U.S.A.

CONTENTS

BOOK TWO
GAMES YOU CAN'T WIN

Harry Anderson — Wise guy

Harry Anderson is either the most interesting guy I've ever known or I'm the dullest guy he's ever known. For whatever reasons a hustler and a ventriloquist get along, we have been the best of friends since the day we met.

Harry's past, like his current television show, is a matter of court record. He was arrested on the streets of New Orleans for playing a game of chance. In San Francisco Harry's jaw was broken by a man who found out that he was not playing a game of chance. The next week, with his jaw wired shut, Harry was back on the street performing the same game. This time, instead of cheating people out of their money, he solicited tips for demonstrating how not to be cheated on the street. The con-man turned consumer protector, the wolf reassuring the sheep.

Some years later I met Harry at the Circus-Circus Casino in Reno, Nevada. We were performing together and Harry was the opening act. It was immediately apparent to me that Harry knew his way around a casino and a circus a lot better than me, so I hung out with him.

During the course of the next couple of weeks, I became part of the Anderson mob. I experienced things that I thought only existed in Dashiell Hammett books. I shilled drinks from Pit Bosses—Harry dealt the cards. I played spectator—Harry worked the shell game. I climbed the trapeze rigging—Harry waved from the floor. I tried to make peace with an obnoxious security guard—Harry picked the guard's pocket and cuffed him with his own handcuffs. I was shot at backstage—Harry held the gun.

We were the last comedy show the hotel ever had. Our show room was turned into a Keno parlor, I was never asked back to the hotel, and Harry was barred from playing cards in the state of Nevada. It was an "interesting" experience.

As a friend and member of Harry's Left-Handed League, I've been a sucker for many of Harry's games. After the fleecing my friend explains the scam and why I can never win. I am constantly amazed that people fall for such tricks, as I reach into my pocket to pay off my bets.

It is highly unlikely that you will ever have a friend quite like Harry. However, the odds are that you may already have a friend like me since, according to Barnum, there is one born every minute. In that case, this book could be worth a lot of money to you.

The unbeatable knowledge that once was shared only with the "league" is now between these pages. It is a collection of the best stuff from Harry's hatful of winning scams.

Someone once said: *"It isn't that Harry is so full of it, it's that he's full of so many kinds of it."*

Photo by John Tenney

"Money is always there,
but the pockets change."

—GERTRUDE STEIN

INTRODUCTION

"Hello, Sucker!"

Winning isn't everything, but losing ain't squat. You want to understand the adult world, watch kids:

I've got a little girl, Eva Fay, who's very bright—learned to play Monopoly when she was only four (and killed herself a bear when she was only three). Learned the rules, the action of play, the whole banana. Now me, I've never been much of one for two-hour games with phoney money, but I'm the Dad (according to the blood tests), so I jump in. I play like a twelve-year-old. Still, Eva plays like a four-year-old, so I win. As Eva began to realize she was losing, she broke down. It was too much for her. She got a slap of the agony of defeat that damn near did her in.

So Eva moves off Ventnor Avenue and on to computer games—not the arcade shoot-em-up kind, but the interactive fiction type where you solve puzzles and problems and the like. She loves these games—she can't lose. Sure, some of the games are tougher than others, and she gets frustrated when she's stuck in a maze, or up against a dragon without a sword, but

Eva's the one playing, so she's the one who's gonna win.

"It's not whether you win or lose . . . it's whether I win or lose."

Maybe it's all the years since my street-hustling days. Playing indoors lets you warm up a bit. Maybe it's the time I've been spending playing a judge on television. Whatever, I've begun to feel something dangerously akin to compassion for the losers of the world. A little of this feeling must have filtered down to Harry the Hat, because I can tell you for a fact that a few years ago he'd never have spilled the beans the way he is doing it in this book.

So what's he up to, besides trying to make a few quick ones from an unsuspecting publisher? Surely he doesn't want a world filled with hustlers. Too many flower-pickers make for a lousy garden. No, it isn't that. I'd venture a guess that the old Hat is trying to help out the unsuspecting—give out the dope that the wise guys figure they've got over everyone else. Yes, I do believe that though the Hat would deny it, this book is a thinly disguised public service—less an ammo dump than a bomb shelter.

So take some advice from an old man. Learn the gags described here, pull them on your pals, keep the bets small. Having them think you a clever sort will mean more to you than the few bucks you can wring out of friends.

On the other hand, you might want to take to heart the lowdown given in the second part—the stuff about those games you should never be playing at all. Learning those lessons yourself is an expensive proposition—you've already spent too much for a paperback—don't go throwing good money after bad.

You know, a very wise guy, Mr. Damon Runyon, once observed:

"Son, no matter how far you travel, or how smart you get, always remember this: Some day, somewhere, a guy is going to come to you and show you a nice brand-new deck of cards on which the seal is never broken, and this guy is going to offer to bet you that the jack of spades will jump out of this deck and squirt cider in your ear. But son, do not bet him, for as sure as you do, you are going to get an ear full of cider."

Me, Turk, and the Hat—we're just trying to help you keep your ears clean.

HARRY ANDERSON

COPYRIGHT © by UNIVERSAL PICTURES, a Division of Universal City Studios, Inc. Courtesy of MCA Publishing Rights, a Division of MCA Inc.

"Never give a sucker
an even break."

—W. C. FIELDS

BOOK ONE

GAMES YOU CAN'T LOSE

"A fool and his money
were lucky to get together
in the first place."
—ANONYMOUS

CHAPTER I

CUNNING STUNTS

HOOK, LINE AND SINKER

I am sitting one day in a local beanery with the old thinkin' hat on as usual—when a very rewarding-type scheme enters my noggin.

Lately, I am frequently noticing that my growing reputation as a notorious sort of character is making the suckers extremely suspicious of even my most honest intentions. I ask one guy for a light and he clamps his hand over his wallet and runs away screaming.

Obviously, the word is out that I will be clever in ways they have never dreamed of and that I will not hesitate one bit to take monetary advantage of the situation. That's right, I been rippin' 'em off something fierce, which is causing John Q. Public to avoid me like a mongrel avoids the dogcatcher.

"Mayhap it is time to turn from fleecing the sheep to tending them." I think. "I am not the only wolf out there. And someone has to give the suckers a more or less fair shake."

It is soon my resolve to grasp one of the less intelligent of the flock and become his professor. How should I put it? To teach him a thing or two.

And if the everlovin' reader, in the process, learns a little about the fine art of games and gaming, all the better.

Thirsty and anxious to embark upon my plan, all I need is a short drink and a ripe sucker. That's easy because the quickest way to get a drink is to find a sucker. And in this joint, as in most bars, there's more suckers than ice cubes.

GO FISH

Fate is with me as who bellies up to the bar but a tall geeky-looking fella named Turk—a prime, grade A, medium-rare sucker. Ya might say he's a cut above the rest.

The first thing you notice about Turk is that his broad grin matches his wide ears almost perfectly. His bright but vacant eyes sort of remind you of a "For Rent" sign. Supposedly we've all been given our own little blessings in life, but this guy makes you wonder.

THE BAIT

"Hey, Turk! Good to see ya pal. In for a little cocktail, are ya? Allow me to sweeten the mix a bit."

Now folks, I am here to tell you that the guy is eyeing me with no small amount of suspicion. Sure, we've made a wager or three in the past and I have to admit that sheer luck forces me to take his cash on every single bet. I try to let him win a couple, just to keep him interested, but this guy can't drop a dime and hit the floor.

Covering his drink with my hat, Lesson One begins.

THE HOOK

"Say, Turk. I'll bet you a buck I can drink that drink without touching the hat."

He ponders the matter a moment before accepting my ludicrous wager by dropping a bill on the bar.

Quick as a wink, I duck my head under the bar and commence with some loud "glunk, glunk" drinking-type noises. Coming back up, I wipe my mouth in a very satisfied manner.

"That's it," say I. "The drink is gone."

"Noooooo," says he.

"Oh yeah, I drank it. Check for yourself."

Now friends, this is the oldest sucker bet in the book, which for his money makes it one of the best. Turk does just what the suckers have been doing since the fedora was invented, which is to pick up the hat and check the drink. At this opportune time, I grasp the drink and quaff it down.

"You lose, Turk! I didn't touch the hat. You did!"

THE LINE

Well, as you might imagine, the poor guy is quickly protesting that anyone can do that trick. Since I disagree we both lay up another buck as the barkeep pours Turk one more. I consider myself to be sporting indeed when I loan him my hat to cover the drink.

"I bet you," he declares, "that I can drink that drink, without touching the hat."

Diving under the bar, the poor fool is "glunk, glunking" for half the day in a performance that will win an Emmy if not an Oscar except that—while he is pretending to drink the drink—I am lifting the hat and really drinking the drink. By the time he comes up for air, the hat is back on the empty glass and only the gathering crowd is any wiser.

"Okay, I drunk it!" claims Turk in a slightly tipsy voice.

Vocalizing my disbelief, I lift up the hat to check. Everyone is amused, but only Turk is downright thunderstruck at the sight of the empty glass.

. . . AND THE SINKER

"That's amazing pal!" say I. "You deserve your buck back. I don't know how you did it, but I'd sure like to try again myself. Is there a hole in the bar or what?

Boy, oh boy-oh, you're getting too good for me, Turk! This time I better only bet you a <u>dime</u> I can drink the drink without touching the hat."

So the barkeep quickly pours the sap one more and covers it with my hat. Normally I am not one to let so many fingers feel my fedora but I make an exception for the sake of educating the masses.

The bet being on, I pick up the hat and guzzle down the drink.

"Aaah! That is refreshing!"

My opponent loudly and correctly protests that I touched the hat.

"When you're right, you're right. You win again! Here's the dime, Bub. I reckon you're just too smart for me."

Turk is looking nine kinds of delighted when the bartender strolls back to his spot and addresses him in a very cool manner.

"Okay pal, that'll be twelve bucks for the drinks."

**"The winners tell stories
while the losers yell deal."**

—OLD GAMBLER'S SAYING

EQUALLY CUNNING STUNTS

The drink under the hat is a simple example of the easiest kind of game you can't lose: the cunning stunt.

Don't be fooled into thinking these are games of chance. <u>You</u> propose the game and <u>you</u> know the secret to winning. In exchange for that somewhat huge advantage, you offer a modest but lively entertainment.

What follows are a few of the most cunning stunts ever.

**"Put on a good show and
they'll be delighted to pay
the price of admission."**

---

1. THE ACROBATIC GLASSES

PROPOSITION: Set three glasses on the bartop, two pointing up and one down. The player is allowed exactly <u>three</u> <u>turns</u> of the glasses. <u>Each</u> <u>turn</u> <u>he</u> <u>must</u> <u>flip</u> <u>two</u> <u>glasses</u>.

The trick is to end up with all glasses pointing up.

Wager that you can **finish** **with** **all** **three** **glasses** **up** even though your opponent, on several tries, will be unable to.

METHOD: Let your opponent go first, gracefully allowing him more than one try. But be certain that, when he begins, the glasses are **two** **up** **and** **one** **down.**

When you begin the trick the glasses must be <u>two</u> <u>down</u> <u>and</u> <u>one</u> <u>up.</u>

(See illustrations for the winning moves.)

ILLUSTRATIONS:
THE ACROBATIC GLASSES

OPENING POSITION FOR YOUR OPPONENT
(2 UP, 1 DOWN)

OPENING POSITION FOR YOU (TO WIN)
(2 DOWN, 1 UP)

FIRST MOVE: Flip #1 & #2

POSITION TWO

SECOND MOVE: Flip #1 & #3

POSITION THREE

THIRD MOVE: Flip #1 & #2

POSITION FOUR

<u>You Win!</u>

---

2. DO AS I DO

Challenge someone to do as you do.

Each of you takes a drink.

You make a gesture with the glass, as "toasting." Your opponent toasts also.

You drink your drink. Your opponent drinks his drink.

You salute with the glass again. Your opponent does likewise.

You spit a mouthful back in your drink. Chances are your opponent has already swallowed.

"Don't assume too much."

3. TOPSY-TURVY MATCHBOXES
(A gaffed "Do as I do")

THE SET-UP: Take two boxes of wooden bar matches from a friendly neighborhood bar and head home for some careful reconstruction.

Remove the trays from each, set the matches aside, and cut the trays in half from side to side. Reverse one of the halves and tape or glue it back to the other so that one end of the tray points up and one end points down.

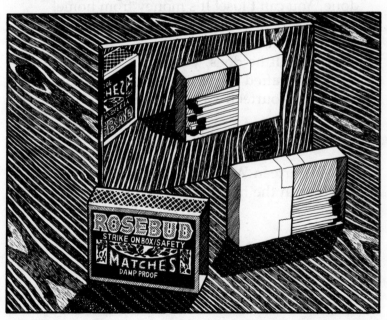

(GAFFED MATCHBOX VIEWED IN MIRROR.)

Replace the gaffed tray into one of the covers, add matches pointing in both directions and head back to your friendly neighborhood bar.

THE CHALLENGE: Toss someone a box of the bar matches, keep the gaffed ones for yourself, and bet that the sucker can't do as you do.

THE MOVES: Flip the matchbox over a few times slowly, so the sucker can repeat your moves.

At any given time you can show your box right-side up. Half of those times, his will be upside down. He hasn't been able to do as you have done. You can't lose! It's money from home!

UNLESS: The sucker wants to examine your matchbox. If he does, you better be able to pull out an ungaffed duplicate or you may receive a visit from Fourteen-Week Freddie.

"Fourteen-Week Freddie?" you ask.

Yeah. Fourteen Weeks: that's the minimum time you'll be in the hospital after Freddie pays you a visit.

4. BALANCING AN EGG ON END

PROPOSITION: To balance an egg on its end.

METHOD #1: You are in a restaurant with some casual acquaintances. During an unobserved moment, lift up the tablecloth and put a little pile of salt on the table, then replace the tablecloth. Offer to wager with your companions that you can balance an egg upright. The egg balances easily when leaned on the small pile of salt beneath the tablecloth.

METHOD #2: No tablecloth? Lick the egg and wipe it off in your palm where you have hidden a little salt. The salt, sticking to the egg, makes a nice base for the egg to lean on.

METHOD #3: No salt? Shake the egg in your hand like a martini, scrambling the yolk and white together inside the egg. Hold it upright for a short time allowing the yolk (the densest part) to sink to the bottom. Gingerly balance it upright. It stays because the heavy part is resting at the bottom.

5. BILLIARDS (BALL BUSTER)

SET-UP: Place two striped balls against the short rail of a pool table. Push them together tightly so that they 'kiss' the rail and each other. Place a solid ball on top so that it rests on the rail and the tops of the two stripes. Easy does it, so they don't roll out.

WAGER: That you can strike the cue ball in a normal fashion from the other end of the table and hit the solid ball (the one on top) without hitting the stripes first.

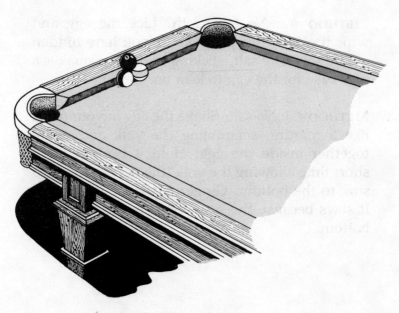

The Set-Up

(The Ball Buster Continued)

METHOD: Softly stroke the cue ball straight at the two stripes. Follow through with a little body English and, when the cue ball is about halfway there, strike your thighs firmly against the table.

The jolt on the table will cause the two stripes to roll apart. The solid ball will fall down between them onto the table where it will be struck by the approaching cue ball.

It's easy. The moving ball directs attention from you. They'll never even see you bump the table.

And if they do, you're still a winner!

6. REMOVING YOUR VEST
WITHOUT REMOVING YOUR COAT
(A Stunt For Three-Piece Bankers)

PROPOSITION: That you can remove your vest (or someone else's) without removing your jacket.

METHOD: With the coat unbuttoned, pull the back of the vest over your head to the front of your body (#1).

Slip the right hand under the coat and under the left shoulder. Grasp the bottom left side of the vest. Push it down into the left sleeve and over the elbow (#2). Then insert the right hand up the left sleeve from the cuff to assist pulling the vest until the armhole of the vest is over the left elbow and, finally, over the left hand (#3).

When the vest is free of the left arm, pull that side back through the left sleeve. All that remains is to slide the whole vest down the right sleeve and out the right wrist to freedom (#4).

(THE REST OF THE VESTLESS)

NOTE: You probably can't win any money at this but you can impress someone with your quick wit and nimble physique.

It might be even more impressive if someone could devise a way to remove their shorts without removing their pants. Of course, it might <u>not</u>. It all depends.

"There'll be a hot, hot time
in Lakehurst, New Jersey
when the Hindenburg lands today!"

—ROBERT SHERMAN & MILT LARSEN

"In a fifty-fifty proposition—
there are some guys who insist
on getting the hyphen, too."

CHAPTER II

PLAYING THE ODDS

THE DOLLAR BILL $WINDLE

"Say Turk, I got another little bet I been workin' on, but I ain't too sure about the odds. Wanna give it a try in the name of scientific research?"

Turk inquires about the cost of said experiment and I respond:

"Oh, a trifling wager—say . . . 20 bucks?"

His coughing fit prompts me to adjust the opening line.

"Okay. That's too high for an afternoon bet. We'll make it a dollar."

At a buck, he's at least willing to hear what the game is.

"It's simple. I take out a one-dollar bill. Like all U.S. currency, this one's got eight digits in the serial number, letters excluded. You try to guess three numbers without missing. Miss one and you lose. But guess just three correctly and you win even money!"

Turk's eyes glaze over as he calculates the variables. There are ten possible digits (0 thru 9) and eight digits on the bill. He only has to guess three. It sounds like a breeze!

Eagerly accepting the wager, he calls out his guesses: three, seven, and eight.

"Darn! You're right!" I say. "They're all here. You win yourself a buck, Turk. I must've miscalculated the odds."

Taking out another one-dollar bill, I offer to try it again.

Turk selects zero, one, and five and I wad up the bill and toss it in his direction.

"You win again," I say. "I guess the bet should have been <u>four</u> digits. Ah well, let's try one more. Shoot! I don't have another ONE-dollar bill. All I got is that twenty I was gonna bet the first time, but you didn't want . . . What's that? You want to go the twenty now? Same bet? Well . . . I guess so. Call 'em out."

He ventures. "Six."

"Nope. No six. You lose. Tough break."

"What the hey. I shouldn't, but I'll give you a second try, double or nothing on the twenty."

"Seven? Uh . . . no. No seven and no six."

The guy is wired in now and he keeps betting and he keeps guessing and he keeps losing.

"Sorry, Turk. There isn't a six, seven, four, three, or a two."

Turk doesn't think this is possible and insists on seeing the bill before paying up. I consider this an insult to my integrity, but display it anyway. What a lucky fluke for me that the serial number on my twenty is: 15511515.

It seems that in all the excitement he neglects to consider the possibility of repeat digits. He protests that with only two digits on the bill he couldn't possibly guess three.

This is an excellent observation Turk has made. On his advice, I may even keep this bill in my wallet in case the bet comes up again sometime. This compliment cheers him up a bit, even as he pays me the hundred bucks.

It seems like a shame to waste such a good bet on an easy mark. Anyone could have been fooled by this simple yet deceptive wager. Here's the true odds on winning.

ODDS:
The Dollar Bill $windle

Guess what? There are eight figures in a bill serial number.

The "caller" must guess three, no misses.

If all figures are different the caller has:
   $8 \times 7 \times 6$ out of $10 \times 9 \times 8 =$ **(336 out of 720)**

(Almost one out of two chances, or nearly even odds. The caller has a slight advantage in this one case, but the chances of a bill not having <u>any</u> repeat numbers are very slim.)

Chances With One Duplicate figure:
   $7 \times 6 \times 5 = 210$ of 720 **(approx. 2 in 7)**

With Two Duplicate Figures:
   $6 \times 5 \times 4 = 120$ in 720 **(1 in 6)**

Three Duplicate Figures:
   $5 \times 4 \times 3 = 60$ in 720 **(1 in 12)**

Four Duplicate Figures:
   $4 \times 3 \times 2 = 24$ in 720 **(1 in 30)**

Five Duplicate Figures:
$3 \times 2 \times 1 = 6$ in 720 **(1 in 120)**

Six Duplicate Figures:
$2 \times 1 \times 0 = 0$ in 720 **(1 in ∞)**
or <u>NAFP</u> (Not a prayer)

**"Logic can never decide
what is possible and impossible."**

YOUR BEST BETS AT PLAYING THE ODDS

One of the greatest areas of confusion in proposition gambling is understanding the difference between chances and odds.

Chances (the sucker's term) are the degree of likelihood of a (favorable) outcome in an uncertain situation.

Odds (a gambler's term) are the probability that one thing will happen rather than another. Or: the exact ratio between the amount to be paid for a winning bet and the amount of the bet.

To the player, blackjack is a game of chance; to the dealer it is a game of odds.

Here's a simple example:

I ask my buddy Turk how often he has coffee with breakfast.

He replies: "Every other day."

The chances, therefore, are 50/50 that he will have coffee tomorrow. The odds are 1 in 2.

That's simple enough but odds can be confusing. Let's take the example one step further.

I ask my good buddy Turk, who is a married type of fellow, how often he makes love with his wife.

In a quiet voice, he admits "About once a week."

I point out that the chances that he will have sex on any given day are 1 in 7. The odds are 6 to 1 against. This does not cheer him in the least.

Being a gambler who likes to work with as much knowledge as possible, I always try to confirm my information before wagering part of my poke (that's bankroll to you rubes).

Posing as a researcher, I knock upon Turk's door one morning while he is at work. His wife answers. I ask a few simple questions of the lady: "How often do you go to a movie?" "How frequently do you eat dinner in a restaurant?" "How often do you have an amorous encounter?"

She answers the last question: "About six times a week."

This is very puzzling. Perhaps what seems like once a week to the husband seems like six times a week to the wife. In light of this conflicting information, I resolve to <u>never</u> gamble on frequency of sex.

However, as I am leaving I pass the mailman, the milkman <u>and</u> the postman carrying their deliveries to the house. And they're all three smiling.

> **"The race doesn't always go to the swiftest,**
> **nor the battle to the strongest,**
> **but that's the way to bet."**
>
> **—DAMON RUNYON**

When trying out the following odds wagers, it'd be worth your while to pay attention to what the numbers really mean. Sure, a good bet at 5 to 4 means it'll work out five times in your favor to four times for your opponent. But that's still four wins for the other guy.

And a 100 to 1 in your favor, is that a sure thing? No, that's what William Cooper was talking about when he said:

> **"A fool must now and then**
> **by chance be right."**

1. UNHAPPY BIRTHDAYS

BET: While discussing the finer points of wagering at a party, an acquaintance notes that there are thirty people present in the room. He offers to <u>wager</u> <u>that</u> <u>two</u> <u>or</u> <u>more</u> <u>of</u> <u>these</u> <u>thirty</u> <u>share</u> <u>the</u> <u>same</u> <u>birthday</u>. Once the bet is agreed upon you will both canvas the room, write down each person's birthday, and compare them for a duplicate.

"Surely," says your friend, "you are willing to wager . . . say ten dollars on this proposition."

QUESTION: Should you take the bet?

You hesitate a bit and your friend states that 30 people out of 365 possible birthdates offers obvious odds in your favor of over ten to one. Being a generous fellow, your friend says he'll bet $15 to your $10, a payoff of 3 to 2 in <u>your</u> favor.

QUESTION: Should you accept the wager now?

ANSWER: No. No way. Unh-unh. Nope. Don't do it.

HOW COME? You believed the odds were about 12 to 1 in your favor (365 birthdates divided by 30 people).

However, you are not wagering on two people sharing one particular birthday (such as yours). You are betting that two people will share <u>any</u> birthday. This is what is known as a progressive calculation. Each additional person adds another set of calculations to the odds.

The fact is, <u>the</u> <u>chances</u> <u>are</u> <u>around</u> <u>fifty-fifty</u> <u>with</u> <u>22</u> <u>persons</u> <u>present</u>. Every added person increases the odds in your opponent's favor so that <u>with</u> <u>30</u> <u>people</u> <u>present</u> <u>the</u> <u>true</u> <u>odds</u> <u>are</u> <u>4</u> <u>to</u> <u>1</u> <u>against</u> <u>you</u>!

Nobody's gonna call you "Sucker!"

2. TWENTY BITS

PROPOSITION: Even though it is obvious, point out that the odds on getting one head from a flipped coin are fifty-fifty. Ask how many heads will most likely turn up when flipping a coin ten times.

"Five out of ten" is the normal reply. Offer 2 to 1 odds against getting *five* heads in ten tosses, then flip away.

METHOD: True, five heads and five tails will turn up more frequently in a ten-coin toss than any other combination (four heads and six tails, six heads and four tails, seven and three, etc.), but the sum of all other possibilities is much greater than the odds for <u>exactly</u> five heads and five tails.

The true odds are five to two in your favor. This means you may sometimes lose but over a period of time you will be a sure winner.

3. THE MATCHING CARD GAME

SITUATION: Two decks of standard playing cards are shuffled and cut to the satisfaction of your opponent. The decks are placed on the table and, using both hands, you turn up one card from the top of each deck simultaneously.

WAGER: That two matching cards (in number and suit) will come up at the same time, one in each hand, before you have gone through the two decks. The assumption made by your opponent is that there are 52 chances to match in 104 cards—an even bet.

TRUE ODDS: The odds are actually about five to four in your favor (20%), not a huge margin, but enough to pull through big in the long run.

EVEN BETTER: Structure the bet so that you win an additional bet for each matching pair and it's like money from home!

REMEMBER: Casinos will play you with <u>much</u> <u>less</u> than 20% odds and just look at their carpeting!

The Matching Card Game
"Another Winner!"

4. ROLL SIX OR EIGHT BEFORE SEVEN

How'd you like to feel like a hotshot craps hustler? There's enough twists and turns in this dice proposition to rattle a snake—or the mark of your choice.

HUSTLER TO YOUR MARK: "Even money that you won't roll a six before a seven—or an eight before a seven. Which do you want?"

Six or eight, it doesn't matter. Both are bad choices—each 6 to 5 against the mark. (Out of 36 possible rolls, there are 6 ways to roll seven and 5 ways to roll six or eight.) If the mark accepts, you've got a proposition with good odds in your favor.

IF THE MARK DECLINES: Offer to switch sides, taking the bet yourself. Furthermore, you'll take it twice over. "Okay!" you say. "I'll choose both six and eight. The bet is that I roll a six <u>and</u> an eight before I roll <u>two</u> sevens."

WHY?: There are 10 ways to roll a five or an eight and six ways to roll a seven. Therefore the odds are 10 to 6 (5 to 3) that you will roll either a six or an eight before his first seven.

Having rolled one, the odds are 6 to 5 against you on your other number coming up before his seven. Your

5 to 3 will win out over his 6 to 5 in the long haul. Keep the bet plugging and you'll clean him out.

AN ALTERNATIVE: If he still won't bet, offer to reverse the whole thing one more time: "Even money you won't roll a six and an eight before two sevens." By now the mark is bound to accept, having had the bet offered to him from all possible sides.

Before you roll the dice, ask which way he wants it: "six-eight or eight-six?" (For six-eight he must roll six first, then eight.)

Now you've sold him your original proposition, twice over—two bets at 6 to 5 in your favor.

CONGRATULATIONS! By fully understanding the odds of your proposal, you've run the mark <u>and</u> his wallet ragged.

5. COINS ON THE TRAY
(A PARTY GAME)

SETTING: So your gathering of friends needs a little life and you could use a bit of change? You propose a game of chance.

GAME: Several people, including yourself, take a crayon and initial the tail sides of all their loose change and dump these coins onto a tray. Someone takes the coins in their hands, shakes them up, and tosses them back onto the tray. All of the coins which have come up heads are then removed and set aside. All of the coins showing tails are taken by another person, shaken, and tossed back onto the tray. This is repeated until only one coin remains. Whosoever initial is on the final coin on the tray is the winner of the game.

BEST OF ALL: The winner keeps all the change. The more coins one puts in, the better their chances of winning, unless you are planning on winning without sweating.

WINNING WITHOUT SWEATING: When you toss your change onto the tray you throw in a 'gaffed' coin—a double-tailed coin that you have purchased at a magic store or novelty shop. Each time the coins are flipped the heads are taken out, insuring that your coin—a tail every toss—will be the last one on the tray.

You win all the change and get your double-tailed coin back.

NOTE: Your gaffed coin should be initialed on one side beforehand. You initial the other side when the game begins.

"Do not believe in miracles, rely on them"

(Gambling addicts wagering on a fly. Note the hard-luck poker hand at the bottom of the poster.)

CHAPTER III

PROPOSITION BETS

ORIGINALITY

There's more to waltzing off a winner than knowing the game. You also gotta leave your victim sufficiently happy or dazed in order for you to pocket the cash.

That's why this chapter is dedicated to Titanic Thompson and Arnold "The Brain" Rothstein, participants in some of the most brilliant and entertaining wagers ever.

Legend has it that "Titanic" Thompson received his peculiar moniker while he was the boss of a gin rummy and poker gambling crew that plied the passengers of luxury steamships traversing the cold Atlantic. The story has it that Thompson, working the Titanic on its doomed maiden voyage, ran his most convincing con ever, dressing in women's clothes in order to secure a seat in a lifeboat.

Truth of the matter is Thompson never worked the lucrative ocean liners. At age 19, he was shooting craps when an onlooker asked the crowd who the hotshot was. No one knew. "The way he's sinking 'em," the curious man said, "he ought to be called Titanic." The name stuck.

Titanic Thompson was the kind of hustler that would wager on which nostril an ugly kid would pick first—and usually win.

Arnold "the Brain" Rothstein, because he could calculate vastly complicated percentages on probabilities and impossibilities, was celebrated in the twenties as the king of the odds. He was also the moneyman behind the rigged 1919 World Series, thrown by the Chicago White Sox, which later came to be known as the "Black Sox" Scandal.

But Rothstein's real mastery, like Thompson's, was an interesting type of wager called the proposition bet. Ti and the Brain didn't originate them but they did make them an art and a science, respectively.

The bets between Ti and the Brain are legend now: the 500-yard golf shot, throwing a walnut over the Potomac, heaving a pumpkin over a three-story building.

Thompson, who was a naturally gifted golfer and played left-handed _and_ right-handed, made only one condition in the 500-yard golf shot: that he name the date and place of his attempt. Guessing that Titanic intended to hit this phenomenal drive off of the Grand Canyon (1600 yards deep), the Brain agreed to the bet on the terms that his opponent pick a level spot.

NOTE: Judging by the number of versions of the story in circulation, this was a bet that Thompson ran on numerous victims. He did indeed also win the bet several times by hitting his drive off a high cliff.

The bet accepted on Rothstein's terms, Thompson ventured onto an icy golf course in the middle of February and smashed a hard drive across the smooth frozen surface of Lake Erie. The ball reportedly didn't stop until the April thaw.

This was a bet so brilliant that Rothstein would have never thought of reneging. Participation in such a deed, even from the money-losing point of view, was the stuff of legends. It still is. When your own sucker walks out of a bar with his cash in your wallet, he ought to feel, not like an idiot, but like a part of something fantastic!

For the purpose of long-distance tossing, Thompson used to carry a couple of peanuts and walnuts filled with lead. The suckers, not being stupid, would select a real nut for the throw, but Thompson—who was adept at switching loaded dice into craps games—would substitute his heavy nut for their light one.

The Brain used his talent for numbers to concoct proposition bets that sounded simple but which the normal sucker just couldn't decipher.

Both Walter Winchell and Damon Runyon reported seeing Arnold in front of Lindy's restaurant in Manhattan wagering on the numbers on the license plates of the passing cars. As you might imagine, the Brain usually won.

Even a Sunday hustler can make a killing with an original proposition bet. Think up a couple of good ones of your own and you've got it made.

Go git 'em! And win one for the Brain!

'37 TITANIC THOMPSON
HT: 6'2" WT: 180 DICE & GOLF: L & R
BORN: ROGERS, ARK. 11/30/92

Ti reigns as the King of the Cons with a 2 G score on a bet that his group would see over 20 white horses during a short train ride. Seems Ti paid a man to stand at a crossing with a triple team of whites.

TITANIC'S MAJOR AND MINOR LEAGUE TAKES

YEAR	MARK	SCORE	BET	METHOD
1903	Tourist	Fly Rod	Rock Fetch	Trained Dog, Planted Rocks
1910	Father	$3,600	Poker	Riffles, Seconds, Crimps
1919	World Champ	$10,000	Horseshoes	Moved Posts Closer
1930	Nick the Greek	$1,000	500 Yard Drive	Hit Golf Ball off Cliff
1934	Byron Nelson	$3,000	18 Holes Of Golf	Shot Honest 29 on Back Nine

'29 THE BRAIN
HT: 5'4" WT: 160 DEALT: L
TOSSED DICE: R BORN: NY, NY

Gotham's premier odds maker, Arnold "The Brain" Rothstein, failing to pay 475 G's lost in a rigged poker game, was sent off to Craps Heaven last year by a slug from a blue-barrelled '38. We'll miss ya!

THE BRAIN'S MAJOR AND MINOR LEAGUE TAKES

YEAR	TEAM	LEAGUE	MARK	SCORE	METHOD
1912	Solo	Bush	Track	$1500	Friendly With the Jockeys
1919	White Sox	Major	Bookies	$350 G's	Bribed 8 World Series Players
1925	Casino	Society	Banker	$320 G's	Owned Crooked Casino
1929	Solo	Tough Guy	Himself	6' Hole	Played With Wrong Guys

A FEW CHOICE
PROPOSITION BETS:

1. Throwing a Walnut

(Across the Potomac)

Thompson and the Brain again. The walnut was full of lead and Ti was quite an athlete.

2. Heaving a Pumpkin

(Over a three story building)

Along with the long golf shot and the walnut toss, Ti made it a legendary three sweep by selecting a pumpkin the size of a baseball.

3. The Fly and the Sugar

Which lump of sugar will a fly land on?

The Brain's Revenge. Rothstein put insecticide on one side of each sugar cube and manipulated them so one spot or the other always faced up.

(This bet may be <u>seen</u> in the 1954 French film "The Sheep Has Five Legs.")

4. Stepping off the Curb

Which foot will a guy step off the curb with first?

This bet is said to be run by watching which side a person favors when walking and carrying objects, but it could also be run with a shill.

That's right: Cheat!

Some guys will bet on anything, but they don't always bet alone.

5. Counting the Pumpkins

Several con men staying at a rural resort would idle away the afternoon on the front porch cutting cards, flipping coins, or making odd bets. Ti, seeing a load of pumpkins go past, mentioned that as a kid he used to load pumpkins and that he could probably guess how many were on the truck, within three. Everyone wanted a piece of that ludicrous proposition.

But they didn't know that, earlier in the day, Thompson had driven past the farmer with the load of pumpkins, chased the fellow down and given him $200 to unload the entire truck and count the pumpkins carefully. Once he had reloaded, the farmer telephoned Ti at his hotel room, reported the total, then drove by the hotel as bait.

After counting the load for the gamblers, the farmer loaded the truck again while Ti loaded his own wallet.

© 1984 Warner Bros. Inc. Photograph courtesy of Warner Bros. Television, A Division of Warner Bros. Inc.

"I told 'em the truth
and they fell for it."

—JUDGE HARRY STONE

CHAPTER IV

TRIVIAL DISPUTE

FLYING IN CIRCLES

How is a good bar like Alzheimer's Disease? Because every day you get to meet such interesting people.

Case in point: a local joint which goes by the name of The Elephant Bar. Yes, the Elephant Bar—where they drink to forget. And where wise guys go to exaggerate their pasts and contemplate the future. Yes, the Elephant Bar—where suckers get stomped flat; at least their wallets do if they start wagering with the smart alecks that hang out here.

There's a variety of things in the bar which will assist in deflating your poke: pool table, poker dice, even a television with tape-delayed sporting events.

And behind the bar they've got Art. He's the resident mixologist. Art keeps a variety of reference books handy to decide arguments about all-time strike-out kings and part-time movie queens. There're copies of the Guiness Book of World Records, the World Almanac, and even a Compact Edition of the Oxford English Dictionary which, weighing in at a very wordy 45 pounds, isn't very compact.

But it does help make for literate hustlers and it's also great for bopping rowdy inebriates on the noggin when they won't pay their tabs and markers. Besides, Art says a dyslectic like himself needs the best dictoinary avialable.

The markers here often add up to elephantine proportions because these guys'll bet on anything; anything, that is, which sounds like a sure thing for the other guy and which can be verified in a handy reference book.

Small fortunes have been won and lost on such simple disputes as: Who was the first black player in professional baseball? (it's not Jackie Robinson.) and Who was the first President of America? (Yes, it's not George Washington.)

Oftentimes our old friend Turk is at the Elephant sipping on his favorite drink, a Hudson River (Ouzo on the rocks). One night his sizeable auditory organs overhear a guy, dressed in an airline pilot's monkeysuit, make an interesting-sounding wager with the sharpest of the sharpers, a fellow known simply as "The Calculator."

As you might imagine, the Calculator is a fellow who knows the odds on practically everything. Without a moment's hesitation, he can tell you that the odds against a craps shooter making a pass on one throw are 1.0286 to 1 and the odds of the same shooter making a run of ten passes are 1023 to 1. Somehow he's still got room in his brain for an amazing compendium of trivial knowledge, a talent which he often uses for the enhancement of his own financial condition.

Everyone in the bar, even Turk, knows this and it is rare these days that the Calculator will find anyone to bet with him around here. Still, he hangs around 'cause he likes being an authority when the bar's record books come up lacking the proper information.

Apparently this itinerant airplane jockey, being new to the neighborhood, doesn't know the Calculator's reputation and enters into the following wager with him: "Which is further from Tokyo, Japan: Minneapolis, Minnesota or Los Angeles, California?"

Well, it is obvious to even the most dense of the crowd at the bar that Los Angeles is about a thousand miles west of Minneapolis and Japan is at least a couple thousand more miles west of the city of Angels. The answer has to be that Minneapolis is further from Tokyo than Los Angeles.

It therefore comes as a huge surprise to all present when Art hands the Almanac to the pilot who finds the pertinent figures and recites them in a loud voice.

"The distance from Tokyo to Los Angeles is 4050 miles. The distance from Tokyo to Minneapolis is 4020 miles. Minneapolis is closer, not further. I win."

Because the gathering observers and sidebetters are buzzing in disbelief, the pilot hands the almanac back across the bar for verification. Art looks closely a moment, then verifies that it's true—4020 to 4050. Los Angeles is further than Minneapolis, Minn. from Tokyo. The Calculator has lost and must pay up the hundred bucks.

The winner gratefully explains the illogic of the bet. This fellow, being an airline pilot, knows that the shortest distance between these cities is not east to west but the great circle route which curves north towards the top of the globe. Minneapolis is far enough north to more than compensate for being further east. The Calculator shouldn't feel dumb because anyone but a pilot would fall for the bet.

Everyone is amazed and impressed. The pilot quaffs a few free drinks and departs with his cash. Our favorite victim, Turk Pipkin, has watched and learned. He has also taken note of the fact that one Harry Anderson, sharper to the world, is nowhere in sight.

A couple hours later, Harry walks into an open trap door and Turk springs the same bet on him. No one in the bar tips pal Harry 'cause Turk has bought their silence with a drink apiece and because they'd all love to see Harry chew on the short end for a change.

Harry naturally accepts the bet, placing his hundred bucks on Minneapolis being further than L.A. from Tokyo. Turk, not a modest winner, shoves the almanac over to Harry.

"Read it and weep, sucker! Revenge is so sweet!"

Reads Harry: "The distance from Tokyo to Minneap-olis is <u>4020</u> miles. The distance from Tokyo to Los Angeles is <u>4005</u> miles. It's only by a gnat's ass but Minneapolis <u>is</u> further. I win!"

"What!? Gimme that book! Damn! He's right. Art! You said L.A. was <u>4050</u>! It's <u>4005,</u> you crook. You took me."

"No-No!" apologizes Art. "I just made a mistake. Everyone knows I got dyslexia. I'm always getting numbers backwards and after that pilot fellow read out 4050, hell, that's what I see on the page. Sorry."

There is nothing for Turk to do but pay and sulk out. His only consolation is that everyone thanks him cheerily for the drinks he has bought.

"Art," whispers Harry. "I am told the Calculator and this dope both lose a hundred bucks because of your dyslexia. Perhaps you should seek professional help."

"Well Harry, it is like this. I get a few phone numbers backwards when wives call for tardy husbands and I even miscalculate my sales tax by the same method once, but my dyslexia is not really acting up much lately. It is just very hard to read the numbers '05' on a page marked by that pilot's <u>50</u> <u>dollar</u> <u>bill</u>! Not often does a guy offer to split a bet with me. The distance just naturally came out as four thousand and <u>fifty</u>.

"Art," says Harry. "You are a very aptly named fellow."

MORE TRIVIAL DISPUTES

Trivialities apply to wagering, as with most categories of bets, when there is a built-in sucker factor.

Once you've posed a question of dispute, you wager on the correct outcome <u>and</u> agree on the source for the information. That source should be one that you have already referred to and one which you both have handy.

Questions of factual knowledge can win you esteem just as often as money. That's okay, because:

_____

"Esteem is often as negotiable as cash."

DISPUTE THESE, WILL YA?

1. Hail to the Chief
   QUESTION: Who was the first President of America?

2. Something Rotten in Denmark
   QUESTION: How do you pronounce <u>Ghoti?</u>
   The answer is a common word.

3. "Day-O! Day-ay-ay-O!"
   QUESTION: Who wrote the Banana Boat Song?

4. Jackie O?
   QUESTION: Who was the first black player in professional baseball?

5. Never the Twain Shall Meet
   QUESTION: Which is further west: Los Angeles or Reno, Nevada?

For answers, see next page.

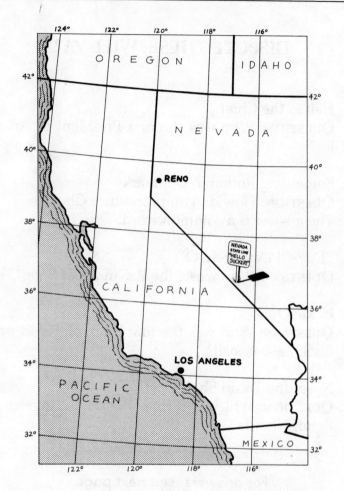

1. John Hancock (1st President of the Continental Congress)
2. "Fish" (*Gh* as in "rough," *O* as in "women," *ti* as in "action")
3. Alan Arkin
4. In 1887, Moses Fleetwood Walker played for Toledo in the International League. (The color barrier, which Jackie Robinson broke, wasn't established until 1888.)
5. Reno, Nevada is in fact west of L.A.

"In the museum of Havana
there are two skulls of Christopher Columbus;
one when he was a baby and
one when he was an old man."

—MARK TWAIN

CHAPTER V

GAMES YOU CAN'T LOSE

THE CONS GAMBIT

(Editor's Note: When we gave him editorial control we didn't expect "the Hat" to insert submissions from other sources. Big surprise: we got conned, too. Harry allows some bozo to write a piece for the book. Here it is.)

Hi! My name is Turk Pipkin. Pipkin not Tipkin. That's a P like in pneumonia. Ha! Ha! That's a joke.

I've got to admit it: this guy Harry is pretty sneaky. So when he said I could describe a contest between the two of us for use in his book, I thought maybe he was trying to <u>rip me off</u>. He's always offering me impossible bets and through sheer luck he usually comes out the winner. Okay, he always comes out the winner, so far.

When he claims he can beat me at any game I choose, it makes me so mad I could just spit. I'll have you know that I play a pretty mean game of golf and I win as much as I lose, almost.

But I select a tougher game than golf 'cause there's no way he can beat me at chess. I attend the weekly chess club meeting and once I even played the state champ and we had a draw game, nearly.

Harry suggested that we play at the chess club and not only did he offer to beat me for a twenty-dollar bet, he also offered to play everybody in the club at the same time and win at least as many games as he lost. Break even against a dozen players at the same time? No way, José!

It was raining out so we only had ten players. But the champ was there and so were the Japanese twins who are so evenly matched that they can never beat each other though they usually romp all over everybody else. Harry didn't have a chance against them and he didn't have much of a chance against me, I thought.

We agreed to not allow draws or resignations. Harry had to play each game out to the end. That way he'd have to think about all the games all the way. That was my idea, I think.

Ten boards were set up in a circle with Harry in the middle. I was at board number one, playing white. Harry played the black pieces on boards one thru five and he played white on six thru ten. That's fair enough, isn't it?

Well, Harry turned out to be a lot better than I figured. White gets to go first so Harry watched my first move and the opening moves of the other white boards, then he made his opening moves on boards six thru ten. After he watched the reply moves on those boards, he came back and moved on one thru five.

The whole match he walked around in a big circle, playing all ten games at once! I couldn't believe my eyes! The guy is some kind of brilliant chess player. He beat me in 17 moves! That was one bet I was <u>happy</u> *to lose.*

Not all of the games were that short but the final outcome was that Harry won four, lost four, and drew two (against each of the twins). He broke even exactly, winning the second bet by a nose! Wow!

(Editor's other note: We think you'll find a better explanation of Harry's chess match in his version which follows. Read on.)

Okay, okay. I never played a game of chess in my life before Turk's challenge. I've got about as much chance of winning a game of chess as a one-legged man has got in a butt-kicking contest.

So, what's the catch? <u>A</u> game of chess I can't win but <u>several</u> games I can break even at and I can choose which of these I'm liable to win and lose.

Here's the rub. I am about as likely to play ten games of simultaneous chess as I am of jumping out of a plane with no chute. In fact, I played no games of chess at all.

What I really play is the "mailman" in five games of postal chess. I take the move played against me on board one and play it on board six. Then I take the reply from six and make that move on board one. I do the same thing on each of the other boards (two against seven, etc.). So we've got five pairs of matching games going. I'm bound to win one of each pair and lose the other—or draw them both. You've never seen chickens dance like these guys when I move just as fast and just as sure as all of them.

The whole time I am grinning to bust a gut because, since I am not playing, I cannot lose. And I don't have to win because I only wager that I will break even, an unlikely prospect if I am in the game but, as it is, a snap!

And the side bet against Turk? How did I know I would win that one game? It's simple: I let Turk play the champ.

MORE GAMES YOU CAN'T LOSE

A TALE OF TWO GREEKS

Once upon a time there was a man called Nick The Greek. Nick just loved to gamble. He'd wager on any and all games, as long as he understood the rules and knew the odds were in his favor. As we'll find out in a few pages, Nick could also <u>steer</u> the odds in that direction.

Then a new Greek came along, one that loved to gamble just as much as Nick, except this Greek could create his own odds. Jimmy the Greek became the odds maker.

This is a book about having some fun with your gaming. Sometimes that means turning the odds in your favor by a little clever gamesmanship. You might try running an overly athletic tennis opponent ragged by cordially hitting the balls back to him for his serve, but accidentally knocking them into his far corner every time. While he's running an extra mile or two picking them up, you'll be driving him crazy with your apologies for being so clumsy.

You can get what you probably want most out of these games: a quick win. And you can do it any-where, most likely picking up a drink or a few bucks in the process. More'n that and you're pushin' it.

You better keep it at a level that's fun, no matter what the outcome, if—like the gambler's dream—you believe that:

It's enough for me
to believe I see
Past the dealer's guard . . .
That
Next
Card.

—NICK THE GREEK (1883–1966)

'**43** NICK "THE GREEK"
HT: 5'10" WT: 210 TOSSES DICE: R
DEALS: NEVER BORN: CRETE, 1883

Last year, Nick "The Greek" Dandolos moved his home base to fledgling gambing burg, Las Vegas, where he busted the bank in one 36 hour non-stop craps game. What's the secret to his sucess? Says Nick: "Coffee!"

THE GREEK'S MAJOR AND MINOR LEAGUE TAKES					
YEAR	LEAGUE	MARK	SCORE	GAME	METHOD
1919	European	Monaco	8 Mil Francs	Roulette	European Wheel
1930	Chicago	Al Capone	$100,000	Craps	Made His Point
1939	Nevada Bush	Art's Casino	$10,000	Chemin de Fer	Held Bank 2 Hours
1943	Major	Sahara	$80,000	Craps	Line & Odds

1. NIM

THE GAME: From a pile of matches two players alternately remove any number of matches up to three. The person taking the last match is the winner.

METHOD: The trick is to count the total number in the pile, then leave your opponent with a multiple of four matches. Whatever number he removes, you subtract from four, removing the difference on your next turn. This again leaves a smaller multiple of four to your opponent. When the pile is down to a total of four it will be your opponent's turn. Whatever number he removes (one to three) will leave three or less matches and you win!

NOTE: *Hustlers at this game often use a pencil to nervously push the matches around when it is their turn. Such 'pencil pushers' are merely slowing things down for a good count of the remaining matches.*

Nim is one of the oldest gambling games known to man or beast. It was played by slaves at the foot of the pyramids of Egypt and later carried thru the Red Sea by the fleeing Hebrews who temporarily abandoned the game because their matches got wet.

It was re-introduced by Benedictine monks in the 13th Century and, through a subsequent increase in match production, helped to end the dark ages.

Smuggled into the New World in the bilges of the vessels of the Spanish Main, it was a back alley game of Nim, not Mrs. O'Leary's cow, which started the great Chicago Fire. The game hitchhiked its way west to infiltrate such notorious gambling towns as Reno, Carson City, and Fresno.

Since it's such an old game there are many different versions of Nim. Sometimes the game is played so that the person taking the last match is the loser! Make sure that you and your mark are playing by the same rules. There are many variations and with any of them it is almost impossible to lose to someone who doesn't understand the secret of the game. This is naturally the reason it has endured so long as a hustle.

Walter Gibson, creator of "The Shadow," exposed the game in a treatise on the subject which was widely circulated among professional gamblers. You'd think that only a rank amateur would subsequently have fallen for the game. Nevertheless, some years later Nick the Greek told Gibson that he had won over $200,000 at Nim because of Gibson's article.

It seems that the Greek had created a subtle little improvement to work on the know-it-alls who thought they understood the game.

Dandalos played along casually enough until the other fellow had him dead to rights with a sure count, then the Greek removed one match on his turn. But, while he removed the one, he secretly added to the pile another match that he had palmed in his hand. This put the count right back on his opponent who likely didn't notice the disadvantage until the last move, at which time he probably figured he had lost the game because he had miscounted early on.

A man who is sure he is about to rip off another is not particularly careful.

"It is easier to be dishonest for two than it is for one."

—JOHN FOWLES

---

2. TIC-TAC-TOE

Here's something to teach your kids so that they'll never lose at this children's game which people play throughout their lives.

As many people already know, you need <u>never</u> lose at Tic-Tac-Toe. This doesn't mean that you can always win. On the contrary, two opponents who fully understand the game and play flawlessly will always tie.

<u>But</u>, since most people don't fully understand the game, it can probably win you a lifetime of free drinks. Here's all ya need to know.

RULES: Tic-Tac-Toe is a game played on a board of nine squares (3 × 3). Each player marks one square alternately. The first to mark three squares in a straight line (horizontally, vertically, or diagonally) is the winner.

HOW NOT TO LOSE
(Playing Second—Wishing to Insure a Draw)

Player "A" (your opponent) can begin by marking in the center, a corner, or on a side.

For "B" (you) to insure a draw:

If "A" marks the center, "B" should mark a corner.

If "A" marks anything else, "B" should mark the center.

(Continuing to a draw from either of those positions is quite simple.)

HOW TO WIN
(playing first)

Number the board as below:

1	2	3
4	5	6
7	8	9

Player "A" (you) may start in two ways and hope your opponent does not know the two rules for "How Not to Lose."

Player "A" (you) mark the center Square (#5).

If Player "B" (your opponent) chooses a side (square #8, for instance), "A" replies with #7, then #4, and you win!

OR:

Player "A" (you) mark a corner (#1, for instance).

Player "B" may respond with #2, #3, #5, #6, or #9. (#4 is same as #2, #7 as #3, and #8 as #6.)

If Player "B" marks #2, "A" replies with #5 and #4. You win!

If Player "B" marks #3, "A" replies with #9 and #7. You win again!

If Player "B" marks #6, "A" replies with #5 and #3. You still win!

If Player "B" marks #9, "A" replies with #7 and #3. Yep. You win again!

3. LIAR'S POKER

THE GAME: Liar's Poker is a popular game played with and for U.S. currency. Two or more players put bills into a pot, the serial numbers face down. Each selects a bill, the serial number of which becomes their "hand."

RULES: Only the eight numeric digits in the serial number are used. **The object is to estimate or guess the total quantity of a particular serial digit on <u>all</u> of the player's bills.** Each person's final estimate is arrived at by a form of bidding.

A "1" is the "Ace" of the game. The ranking of the digits in order from lowest to highest is: 2, 3, 4, 5, 6, 7, 8, 9, 0, 1.

BIDDING: A person may bid any amount he wishes without regard to the hand he is holding. If the first bidder is holding serial #24417831, he might logically bid "two 4's" or "two aces." If he wishes, he may bid "six 9's." The game is called <u>Liar's</u> Poker.

In clockwise rotation, each subsequent player must bid higher than the previous bid, or must "pass." When everyone has passed except the last person to bid, the bills are compared to determine the winner.

THE WINNER: If the last bid does exist on the total bills, then the player who made the bid is the winner, keeping all of the bills from the hand. Five players in a game with one-dollar bills results in a <u>profit</u> of $4 to a successful final bidder.

If the final bid is not present on the bills, that player pays each of the other players. Five players in a game with one-dollar bills results in a <u>loss</u> of $4 to a final bidder who has overestimated the total.

Each player then draws another bill from the pot and another round begins. This continues until the ante is exhausted.

THE BILLS: The honesty of Liar's Poker is dependent upon two things: first, that the players use bills which are not readily distinguishable from one another and second, that the players have not studied the serial numbers on the bills. Well circulated currency with particular distinguishing marks are not normally used, nor is new currency.

STRATEGY: The goal is to exactly guess the total of a particular digit or to cause one of the other players to overbid.

Information on guessing the exact total is compiled from your own hand, from intelligent guesses on when the other players are bidding truthfully, and from an understanding of the odds of any number appearing in a particular quantity.

In a six-handed game, there are forty digits which you cannot see. Among the other hands, on the average, four of a particular digit will occur more often than any other total (similar to the flipping of a coin ten times), but the possibilities of the digit appearing two, three, five, or even six times are also very high.

CHEATER'S POKER: Players may have memorized the serial numbers on bills that they toss into the pot. They may also have marked the back of these bills so that they can draw an unusual bill (ex: six aces) for their own hand or so that they may know which bills are held by the other players.

A player with a weak memory may obtain new bills from the bank. These bills have serial numbers in sequence, making it possible to easily memorize all of your own bills in the pot. New bills are prematurely aged by putting them through the washing machine, after which time the opponents are hung out to dry.

4. GOLF

COURTESY: Golf is a game in which the players are notoriously sensitive to rude distractions such as coughing in backswings, standing with your shadow on the hole and passing gas while they putt.

This is exactly why you <u>shouldn't</u> resort to these odious tactics. Remember that your opponent is carrying a bag full of steel clubs <u>and</u> wearing steel spikes on his shoes. Besides, golf is one of the few games where courtesy is considered a rule rather than a social obligation.

If you really want to get someone's goat in the world's most frustrating game, compliment them on their bad shots with genuine admiration. Blame all your own good shots on luck and your bad ones on misfortune.

Your opponent will be lucky to break a hundred.

DISTANCE: Can't get the distance you need out of your irons in order to whup the local snot-nosed braggart? Try rubbing a thin coat of Vaseline on the club face. It's an old golf hustler's trick and it'll add about 10 yards to your long approach shots <u>and</u> make them straighter.

To a golf fanatic, the explanation for this unusual phenomenon is almost as interesting as the trick. The vaseline lengthens the contact time between the club face and the ball, imparting more forward momentum and less side spin to the ball.

It's illegal, so don't try it in a tournament and don't publicize what you're doing in a friendly money match. Vaseline can be applied quite slyly and cleanly from a squeeze tube, available from your friendly pharmacist. Don't get the Vaseline on your hand, glove, or grips or you may be throwing the club farther than you hit the ball.

Fore!

5. CHESS

Here's the scoop on how to protect your public image if you're challenged to a game of chess by someone who wishes to ridicule your ignorance of the game.

You don't even need a full knowledge of the workings of the game. Simply head down to the local bookstore where you purchased this fine volume and peruse one of their books on Chess.

You'll find, in a chapter on "Chess Openings," some classic openings—or series of moves—with intimidating names like the Giuco Piano and the Greco Counter Gambit. Memorize the first four or five moves of one of these openings and head for your match.

All you need do is begin the game, playing the moves you have memorized. As you move, compliment your opponent on his "strong control of the center" and his "early development."

After his fourth or fifth move, study the board for a bit, then resign, saying: "You've obviously been studying the new Counter Gambit Variations. I can see that you're too good for me. I resign. Good game! Really great! It was my pleasure!"

He wins but you garner the respect of the onlookers (and probably your opponent) as being the more knowledgeable player.

"Lose magnificently, or not at all."

Book Two

GAMES
YOU CAN'T
WIN

"I'm telling you Bud
your name will be mud
if you ain't got that
ace in the hole."

—Diamond Spike

Photo by John Tenney

"Behind every great fortune,
there is a crime."

—HONORÉ DE BALZAC

INTRODUCTION

(Editor's Note: The following was transcribed from a tape recording of a telephone conversation between Harry "the Hat" Anderson and one Turk Pipkin, pigeon. The tape was obtained through normal government channels.)

RING, RING.

H.A. "YO. IT'S YOUR NICKEL. START TALKING."

T.P. "HARRY! DID I PASS THE COURSE?"

H.A. "I DON'T KNOW. WHAT DID YOU EAT?"

T.P. "HA HA. I MEAN THE SCHOOL FOR SUCKERS, DID I PASS?"

H.A. "OH YEAH! YOU'RE THE NUMBER ONE DOPE IN YOUR CLASS.

T.P. "GEE, THAT'S GREAT!"

H.A. "AND DON'T THINK I'M NOT GRATEFUL FOR ALL THE FINE WORK YOU'VE DONE PLAYING THE SUCKER."

T.P. "GRATEFUL."

H.A. "OF COURSE! I KNEW ALL ALONG YOU WERE ONLY ACTING STUPID."

T.P. "ACTING . . . RIGHT."

H.A. "SURE! JUST TO HELP ME OUT WITH MY LITERARY PROJECT OF EDUCATING THE MASSES. FACT OF THE MATTER IS, I'M ALL SET TO PAY YOU FOR YOUR WORK."

T.P. "PAY?"

H.A. "WELL, NOT <u>PAY</u> IN THE TRADITIONAL SENSE, BUT <u>PAY</u> IN THE MUCH BETTER SENSE. I'LL STAKE YOU TO A BIG WIN AT THE GAME OF YOUR CHOICE. YOU CAN CHOOSE ANY PLACE YOU LIKE TO TAKE OFF A BIG PIECE OF CASH USING <u>ONE HUNDRED BUCKS</u> OF MY MONEY!"

T.P. "A C-NOTE?"

H.A. "RIGHT. THIS WILL DEMONSTRATE THAT MY COURSE REALLY HELPS YOU GET WISE AND IT'LL SHOW LOTS OF FOLKS HOW EASY IT IS TO MAKE A LITTLE HONEST CASH—ONCE THEY KNOW THE ROPES."

T.P. I'M ALL EARS.

H.A. DAMN NEAR!

T.P. HUNH?

H.A. SO, WHERE YOU GONNA RISK THE MONEY?

T.P. NO DOUBT ABOUT IT: LAS VEGAS!

H.A. VEGAS?!

(CLICK. DIAL TONE.)

T.P. "HELLO. HARRY? HELLOOO . . . OPERA-
TOR . . ."

Photo by John Tenney

"It looks the same
as we used to play
in WW I."

—GEORGE BURNS
Going in Style

CHAPTER I

CASINOS

THE MAN IN THE BATHROBE

The in-laws had given them a hundred bucks to gamble during their honeymoon in Vegas and they'd pretty much pissed it all away. It didn't take long.

Twenty dollars bought ten rolls of nickels for the slots, a guaranteed 400 pulls—more than most couples get on their honeymoon. An hour later they were nickel-less and Susan's arm was tired.

Looking for a cocktail lounge, they found a Keno parlour. No matter, the drinks were free and the girl in the short dress showed them how to play one Keno ticket nine ways. If the Ping-Pong balls with the right numbers came up, they could win $20,000!

Unfortunately, their nine-dollar card had lost eighteen ways by the time the drinks arrived, so they set off in search of some real gambling. If they'd wanted to play bingo, they could've stayed at the church.

What they found next was risk in one of its purest forms: a wheel, covered in money. Beneath it was a layout where one could place bets on which bill the wheel would stop on.

Their first bet didn't win so John got bold, pulling fifty dollars from the remaining fifty-five in their stake, betting it on the twenty spot. The wheel came up a joker and the man took their money.

Crud! thought John.

"Crap!" said Susan.

Their last five-dollar chip they decided to keep as a souvenir to show the grandkids. That was such a good idea that the newlyweds went directly up to their room to make some grandchildren.

They fell asleep during Carson's monologue.

John awoke to the test pattern and turned the TV off with the bedside switch but he just couldn't keep his eyes closed. The all-night Las Vegas neon was too bright.

"But wait!" thought John, sitting up with wide eyes. "The curtains are closed. That red light is coming from <u>inside</u> the room! Yes! There on the dresser—glowing!"

He got up to investigate.

It was the five-dollar chip, glowing red, etching the vision of a red five on his retina, deep into his brain.

A strange expression came over John's face. Quietly he put on his bathrobe and slippers, took the warm chip in his hand and slipped out the door.

On the casino floor no one paid much attention to the man in the bathrobe. If they had, they would have noticed that he was searching for something.

"Hey! Over there!" his mind screamed. "The red five on the roulette layout is glowing—just like the chip in your hand. It must be a sign from God!"

Twenty steps and he's at the wheel. The man in the bathrobe places the five bucks on the glowing five. The wheel spins one way, the ball the other until it dips down, bounces once and sucks into the red five.

"Five. A winner!"

Roulette pays 35 to 1 on a straight-up number bet. The grandkids' five bucks is suddenly $180. The man in the bathrobe, listening to the beat in his head, like fingers snapping to time, lets it ride.

Snap. Snap. Snap. Snap.

The wheel goes one way, the ball goes the other and they meet at red five. The pit boss asks if he wants the $6480 in cash or chips.

Snap, snap. Snap, snap.

No matter, he wants to bet it all again.

But there's a $500 table limit, so the bet is declined. John stuffs the cash into his robe pocket and walks out into the summer night. It's hot and still. The static electricity in the air makes the hair on his arms stand on end.

Snap, snap. He still hears . . . snap, snap . . . that music.

An hour later. A man in a bathrobe walks up to the Horseshoe Club, a no-limit house downtown. At 4:00 a.m. Fremont Street is lit brighter than the daylight. The heat from the electrified desert air and the million light bulbs comes in with him. A person looking closely might see his head jerking slightly to a strange beat. In a daze he surveys the room.

"There it is! At the roulette table in the corner. Look at the five. It's glowing!"

And you know that the man in the bathrobe can't do a single thing in the world except bet it all, $6480, on five.

Snap, snap. Snap.

The dealer, sweat soaking through his shirt, prepares to roll the ball. The Pit Boss is looking over his shoulder. Neither of them see the glowing five or hear the beat.

Snap, snap. The man in the bathrobe hears it.

The ball leaves the dealer's hand and dives directly into red five—without even spinning around the wheel.

"Five," calls out the dealer grimly. He's probably gonna lose his job and he doesn't sound too happy. The $6480 has just grown into $233,280. From the small crowd gathering round the winner, a guy asks what he's gonna do with all that money.

John doesn't hesitate. He wants to let it ride.

The odds on hitting any number four times in a row are over ten million to one. <u>If</u> the house takes this bet <u>and</u> loses, the man in the bathrobe will be paid $8,398,080!

The Pit Boss consults with the shift manager who calls up the owner. It's really hot in the casino now, like an electric sauna. The house boys are all covered in sweat.

John looks cool in his bathrobe. On the layout, for John's eyes only, is a glowing five. Snap. Snap.

More for the casino's guarantee than for John's, the wheel is lifted off, its mechanism examined for magnets or gimmicks. It checks out fine and the casino accepts the bet.

Snap, snap.

Round and round and round she goes, where she stops, only the ball knows. One sound: the ball, rolling and rolling and rolling round the track. The graveyard slot fiends and the all-night crap shooters have stopped and gathered into a crowd. They've all calculated the eight-million-plus payoff and a few are trying to figure how to get some of it. The ball spins a little slower now, dips toward the numbers, bounces twice and lands squarely in red five!

Wow! He's done it! Un-be-liev-able!

Then it hops back up and lands next door in black 22.

Snap.

"22!" says the man at the wheel, breathing a sigh of relief.

"22?" says John. The red five winks at him once, then the glow fades. The smiling five suddenly looks like a smirking face.

John just walks out, heading back to his bride. The air is cool now. It smells fresh, like rain. At the hotel he gets on the elevator and pushes five.

When he slips in, his bride awakens. She asks him where he's been.

"I couldn't sleep. I went down to the casino to gamble."

"How'd you do?"

"Oh," he says. "I lost five bucks."

CASINOS

How They Make Money

GIVE IT YOUR BEST SHOT

As the man in the bathrobe found out, it's all in your point of view. Casinos can be as fun or as terrifying as you make them. They've created an environment that lets you make it what you will—as long as you don't try to will up some guaranteed free money.

They can make you so happy that you'll pay $45 to see Tony Orlando and <u>like</u> it. Or they can make you so desolately sad that the hotel room windows don't open above the third floor.

So listen up; if you want to have some mindless fun, go to Las Vegas or Atlantic City and let the casinos entertain you as they grind away at your bankroll with the house percentages—if you want to have some mindless fun.

But, <u>if</u> you want to be entertained and <u>perhaps</u> make a little of the long green while you're there, treat your trip like a big-game hunt. You've got to prepare well because these guys are animals. Make a plan. Stick to it. If it fails, you can regroup for the next trip.

So browse through the upcoming explanation of the best and the worst of the casino games and apply the following rules to your strategy.

Happy hunting, Bwana.

"A little of this city goes a long way."

—DR. RAOUL DUKE
("Fear & Loathing in
Las Vegas")

CASINO DO'S AND DON'TS

1. **Don't** risk more than you can afford to lose.
(Don't take credit cards and checks to the gambling floor with you. Decide well in advance what you can afford to lose.)

2. **Don't** get drunk while you're gambling.

3. **Don't** play games that you don't understand.

4. **Do** make wagers that provide the Casinos the smallest winning percentage.
(A smart gambler will find these bets at both the craps layout and the blackjack table.)

5. **Do** bet conservatively when you're losing.
(Don't "chase" your losses.)

6. **Don't** bet heavier when you're winning.
(Don't fall for the notion that you're ever gambling with the house's money. When they pay a bet, it becomes your money.)

7. Be lucky! Be a winner!

1. SLOT MACHINES

By ringing a bell during feeding time a psychologist once trains a dog to sit up, roll over, play dead, and answer the phone. Finally the dog gets so full and so fat from all the feedbag that he won't perform anymore.

So the doc puts the dog on a serious diet, having him perform just as many tricks as ever but feeding him randomly, only after every ten or even twenty tricks. In no time at all the guy discovers that the pooch is once again sitting up, rolling over and is now answering the phone even when it isn't ringing.

If you've played the slots till you were as mad as Pavlov's dog, you're not alone. Slot machines are now Las Vegas' biggest money-maker! That makes them John Q. Public's biggest money loser, partially because they can't know what the odds against them are. As you've always suspected, the odds vary radically from machine to machine.

In Atlantic City the house percentage (P.C.) is limited by law to 17%, a huge house advantage! (Meaning that 17¢ of every $1.00 inserted stays with the casino.)

In Nevada there is no law that limits the house percentage at slots! It's legal for the casino to put in a slot that pays off once every ten years, but it's not very good for business, so most of them are set to grind away, just as surely but a little more slowly, at your stake.

NOTE: Don't play the slots at the airport, the grocery store, or the beauty salon. These locations don't depend on repeat business and their machines have the worst odds in town.

NOTES: There's no change in the odds on a machine that has just paid off <u>or</u> on a machine that's been "cold" for a long time.

TIP: Some nickel machines offer the house around a 10–15% advantage (in Nevada) but <u>some</u> of the dollar slots <u>may</u> offer a house P.C. as low as 2 or 3%. That's still a disadvantage to you, though, and you're now losing twenty times as much per pull, but it's a lot better shake than the wrong side of 15%.

TIPS: Tip the gorgeous girl who gives you your change and ask her which is a hot slot. Maybe you'll get lucky!

2. KENO

Keno is a game in which the sucker marks one to fifteen numbers on a card numbered from 1 to 80. The casino selects twenty numbers at random and, if a high enough percentage of the numbers marked by the sucker are also drawn by the casino, the sucker wins "miracle money"—so named because only a blind saint could accumulate much of it.

These aren't odds, they're a joke—so funny that the Atlantic City casinos aren't even allowed to operate the game. The Nevada Gaming Commission, knowing who is the butt of the joke, allows Nevada casinos to run the game and keep one quarter of the money wagered on the game each year. At 25%, the house P.C. is the highest of any game on the strip.

On the other hand, Keno is the only casino game that you can play while you do something worthwhile; eat a meal, balance your books, or write a letter home for more cash.

Look at it this way. Figure it takes ten minutes to play a game of Keno. There's no other Casino game you can play constantly for an hour, only drop six bucks, and still have a chance, however slim, of winning big. Besides, the Keno runners are cute and friendly and don't have pit bosses looking over their shoulders when they talk to you.

So if you're inclined to drop a couple of bucks on the game to see how your luck is running, go ahead. Beyond that I'd suggest simply asking for the manager of the casino and handing him a fourth of the money in your wallet, sucker!

3. ROULETTE

Roulette is a glamour game for ladies and a gentlemen's game for the guys. It's a touch of class. It's got a nice sound as the ball goes around and you don't <u>have</u> to know anything to play.

WHAT YOU <u>SHOULD</u> KNOW

The American Roulette wheel has 38 numbers: 1 thru 36, 0 and Double 0.

You may place many different bets including: the single-number bet (pays 35 to 1), two-number bet (pays 17 to 1), three-number bet (pays 11 to 1), four-number bet (pays 8 to 1), five-number bet (pays 6 to 1), and a twelve-number bet (pays 2 to 1).

You may also wager on numerous even-money bets concerning whether the ball will fall in red, black, odd, even, 1–18 or 19–36.

This gives you a lot of ways to lose your money because the house percentage on each of these bets, with only one exception, is 5 5/19 percent.

0 and Double 0 are the big catch. Sure, you can bet on either of them and they pay the same as any other number, but the fact that there are 38 possible num-

bers makes the 35-to-1 payoff a definite losing proposition.

And what is the one bet that is an exception to these odds? The five-number bet (0, 00 and 1, 2, & 3) which ups the house percentage to a whopping 7 17/19! This saves you a lot of time because you lose your cash much faster.

HINT: A couple of Nevada casinos (The Cal-Neva Club in Reno and the Hilton and Tropicana in Vegas) may have a European wheel with only <u>one</u> zero. This cuts the house edge to 2.70! Look for 'em. Use 'em while they're hot!

HINT: You might play the number that just came up. Maybe it's a faulty wheel that favors a particular area. It's unlikely, but that number is as good as any other.

DID YOU KNOW?

Thanks to Sean Connery, black 17 is the most commonly played number. Why? Because that's the number James Bond, 007, always plays.

I FEEL IT IN MY BONES

Roulette appeals to many psychics who believe that the motion of the ball can be controlled by mental forces. There might be hope for us all. Perhaps Elvis will help us choose the right numbers.

4. MONEY WHEEL

{(The Big Six Wheel)}
(P.M. Wheel)

Any game with so many names must have been cursed pretty often by losing gamers who play because the Money Wheel is so simple that anyone can understand the thing—even a sucker.

A large vertical wheel has been divided into 54 sections which are covered by U.S. currency: ones, fives, tens, and twenties. There's also one joker and a casino logo or "bug."

The player lays a wager on one of the sections, the wheel is spun and anyone having money down on the winning number collects. The one-dollar bill pays 1 to 1, the five pays 5 to 1, etc. The joker and casino logos pay 40 to 1, cold hard cash. And it'll be a cold day in Vegas before you win much hard cash here.

TRUE ODDS: The Vegas house percentage ranges from 11.1 for a one-dollar bet (24 one-dollar sections out of a total of 54) to a whopping 24 percent on the joker and logo (1 each out of 54 sections).

THE BIG SIX (or Pari-Mutuel): Big Six is a similar game in which the wheel and layout are covered in combinations of three dice. The wheel looks a little more sophisticated but the odds are just as crude.

HEY! If you insist on wagering on these high percentage games, at least check to see that the number on the felt that you cover with your money also appears on the wheel. I once saw just such a mismatched wheel and layout. The house odds on the bet? One hundred percent!

WHY DOES ANYONE PLAY THESE GAMES?

Perhaps because they're so much easier for the novice gambler to understand than craps or blackjack. And that's who it's there for: novice gamblers. If that's what you are, have fun . . . but don't be surprised if some games treat you like a rookie.

5. CASINO POKER

The casino deals the cards and collects 10% of each pot from gamblers who play each other in Hold'em, Seven Card Stud, or Razzle.

Only three small problems get in the way of a profitable, fun time.

PROBLEM #1. Possibly up to four of the players at a table may be employees of the casino (and two of those may be playing with casino money). Luckily, Nevada gaming rules require the casino, if asked, to identify which, if any, of the players are working for the house.

"It's hard to bluff a guy who isn't gambling with his own money."

PROBLEM #2. Besides some very experienced and honest local pros in the games, there are also occasional teams of outside cheats who use signals and codes to exchange information about their own hands and to plan betting strategies that may box you in.

**"Never play poker with a guy
who does card tricks."**

**"Never do card tricks for the group
you play poker with."**

PROBLEM #3. If you're winning, the house is raking in <u>your</u> money. Poker is not a game of chance, it's a game of money. If you like poker, play at home.

**"Casino Poker is to poker,
as military intelligence is to intelligence."**

6. CRAPS

(ALMOST A FAIR SHAKE)

Take My Advice, Please

Not just complete books, but entire libraries have been written about playing both craps and blackjack. Some of those books are invaluable. Others are crap and bust, respectively. Take their advice (and mine, and everyone else's) with a single grain of salt and a couple of cross references and your wallet will be fatter for it.

The Spirit of the Bones

Besides having the most appropriate name of any casino game, craps also provides maximum excitement for your money and some of the best odds of any casino game, if you know how to bet.

Plus you get to handle every prop except the stick that pushes the dice to you. The game has a down-and-dirty smell to it and you get to call the dice "bones" or "ivories." A game like this, ya gotta love!

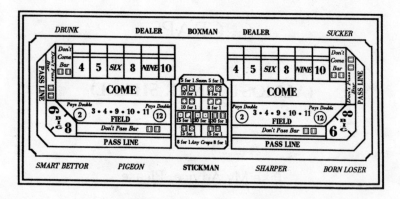

The Basics of the Game

1. The roll of the dice is rotated among the bettors. When the dice are offered to you, choose two from the five that the stickman slides towards you. Throw the dice hard enough to bounce off the rail at the opposite side of the table.

2. Your bets will be paid or collected by the dealer. When the dealer pays off a winning bet, pick up the chips or they may become a bet on the next throw.

3. The shooter's first toss of the dice is the "come-out" (as is each throw after a decision has been made).

4. If the come-out roll is a two-dice total of 7 or 11 (a "natural"), the shooter has a winning decision: a "pass."

5. A come-out roll of 2, 3, or 12 is a losing decision: "craps."

6. If the come-out is 4, 5, 6, 8, 9, or 10, that number becomes the shooter's point and the shooter continues to throw until he wins by throwing his point again (a pass) or he loses by throwing a seven.

The Bets & The Odds

1. **The Pass Line:** A wager that the shooter will pass (throw a natural on the come-out or repeat his point before rolling seven). The bet pays even money (1 to 1). The house P.C. is 1.414 or 14 cents on ten dollars.

2. **Don't Pass Line:** A wager that the shooter won't pass (craps on the come-out or seven before rolling the point). Pays even money at a 1.402%, almost exactly that of the pass. Note: Two sixes (sometimes two aces) on the come-out roll result in no action with don't-pass bets.

3. **Come Bet:** A wager that the shooter will pass, the next roll to be considered a come-out roll. (If the shooter throws a natural, you win. Craps, you lose. Any other number becomes your point and the dealer will move your bet to that numbered box.) Come bets pay even money at a house P.C. of 1.414.

4. **Don't Come:** A wager that the shooter won't pass, the next roll to be considered a come-out roll. Pays even money at 1.402. (Also bars payoff on 6–6 or 1–1.)

The Sucker Bets
(the center of the layout)

(It doesn't matter what these wagers concern. Look briefly at the odds and then never consider these bets again!)

1. **Big Six and Big Eight:** Pays even money with a 9.9 P.C. Ouch!

2. **The Field Bets:** Pays even money with a P.C. of 11.11%. Pow!

3. **Hardway Bets:** Pays 7 to 1 or 9 to 1 with house odds of 11 1/9% or 9 1/11%. Socko! Bam! Boom!

4. **Come-out Bets:** Even though they pay 7 to 1 to 30 to 1 the house P.C. varies from 11 1/9 to 16 2/3. Down for the count!

Note: Avoid the temptation. If necessary, stand at the long ends of the table where you can't reach the center of the layout. When you play these bets, every wise guy at the table knows you're a sucker, a drunk, or both.

Free-Odds Wager

Taking the odds or the "Free-Odds Wager" is the craps shooter's best bet.

If you make a pass bet and the shooter rolls a number on the come-out, you are allowed to make an additional bet (equal to the first) that the shooter will make his point. The bet pays at absolutely <u>true</u> odds with no house P.C. (A point of four [or ten] pays 2 to 1 because there're 6 ways of rolling seven and 3 ways to roll four. A point of five or nine pays 3 to 2 and a point of six or eight pays 6 to 5.)

Since the casino pays correct odds on these bets— with NO house percentage—a pass line bet in combination with your free-odds bet reduces the total odds against you to a <u>0.84 P.C.</u> And that's what ya been looking for all along!

It's such a good deal that there's no space marked on the board for free odds bets. Instead you have to "know" to place your odds bet directly behind your pass line bet.

TIP: Some casinos now allow bettors to make substantially larger free odds wagers, offering double-, triple-, or higher-odds wagers. This can be to your advantage but it can also bust your bankroll fast on a cold streak. Don't multiply your odds bet. Instead, divide your line bet and you'll have better odds with the same money riding.

NOTE: The free-odds bet can also be placed by the don't-pass (or "wrong") bettor. If you add up the house percentages to the third decimal, the wrong bettor enjoys a very slight advantage over the right bettor. The pressures, however, from the right bettors may make you want to play at 3:00 A.M. when the rest of the wrong bettors usually crowd the table, betting against the shooter.

CONCLUSION: Take the odds and run. Even though the house percentage is much smaller than at most casino games, it's still against you on every bet. So why do so many people flock to the craps tables? Because, Bucko, you get to shoot the dice. And there ain't nothing like it!

7. BLACKJACK

(HARD WORK, GOOD ODDS)

Here's a game where skill can dramatically shift the odds in your favor.

The Basic Casino Game
(What You Should Already Know)

Each player and the dealer receive two cards. The total numerical value of the two cards is added (face cards count 10 and aces 1 or 11). Each player plays against the dealer's total, the winner being the hand closest to 21 without going over.

A blackjack (natural "21") pays 3 to 2, unless the dealer also has one, in which case you tie and no money changes hands.

You can double down by turning both cards up and adding an amount equal to your original wager in exchange for one more card (& one only). Note: Some casinos only allow a double down on certain numbers.

You can split two cards of the same value, adding a second wager equal to the first and receiving a second card on each of the split pair. Each of these hands are then played normally, the first hand thru, then the second.

The dealer must draw to 16 and stand on 17.

Some Other Things
(You Might Not Have Thought About)

Insurance, offered by the dealer when he has an ace showing, is always a bad bet (5.88 P.C. except with a blackjack).

Never insure a blackjack, either! The house P.C. is 8.16 and you lose your 3-to-2 payoff!

Always split aces and eights and never split fours, fives, and tens.

When you have a soft hand (an ace gives you two possible totals ten points apart):

Only an unfleeced sheep stands on soft 17 or less.

Stand on soft 18 against dealer's show card of 9, 10, or ace.

Always stand on soft 19 or 20.

Card Counting

Unlike any other game in the casino, what happened on the previous roll (or spin or deal) does affect the following hand. If you can keep relative track of which cards have been dealt, then you have information which can increase your odds by helping you adjust the amount you bet and whether you should take additional cards.

However, card counting, which is not easily learned, must become second nature for you to do it quickly enough to adjust your strategy deal by deal. If you buy one of the many available books on card counting, keep in mind that much more money has been lost by would-be card counters than has been won by those who were successful.

Card Counting for Dyslexics

If you can find one, play a single-deck game and watch the cards as they're dealt. If a lot of tens have come out of the deck, it's a weak deck and you should cut your basic wager in half. Conversely, if a lot of twos thru sixes have been dealt, it's a strong deck and you should double your standard bet.

That means your standard bet must be an amount you can halve or double. For instance, you might play on a two-dollar minimum table where your standard bet would be $4, your strong-deck bet is $8 and your weak-deck bet is $2.

This type of counting won't bust the house percentage, but it may reduce it a little and let you take better advantage of a lucky streak.

BUT DON'T FORGET: If the casinos have made more money off of would-be counters than successful counters, think how well they must have done with haphazard losers who think they've got the game all figured out.

Casino Gambling In Short

There is a right way and a wrong way to gamble. Since the odds are almost always against you, at least give yourself the best chances available and hope that Lady Luck will see you through.

FOR MORE INFORMATION: On how to play these casino games, how to improve the odds in your favor and how to play the games we haven't mentioned like baccarat, high-low, or off-track betting, call, go by, or write to:

> The Gambler's Book Club
> 630 South 11th Street
> Box 4115
> Las Vegas, NV 89127
> 1-800-634-6243

And tell 'em Harry sent ya!

As you learn your betting systems, your card counting, and your magic spells, remember . . .

"There are no non-profit casinos."

Get it?

CHAPTER II

THE CARNIVAL

Photo by John Tenney

"He was a courtly, charming citizen,
presently on parole."
—THE AMERICAN CONFIDENCE MAN

THOSE THREE LITTLE
MILK BOTTLES

"Gee, Harry! Casino gambling sounds a little too complicated for me. I better try some marks that are a little less sophisticated. I know: the carnival! Those rubes will be easy."

"Ah yes, those rubes."

"A few years back, I was in this little town about twenty miles west of San Diego and this burg was s-l-o-w, slow. So I decided to check out the visiting entertainment, the Mole Brothers Carnival, which was set up in a little field on the edge of town."

"I'm standing around, just minding other people's business, when an attractive shape happens by and I just cannot turn my gaze away."

"Now I am always one to need glasses for matters such as settling wagers on the number of hairs on a hirsute mole, but I am blind and stupid too if I do not fall for this doll."

"However, hanging onto her arm is a big clown sporting a well-worn letter jacket and I take it by the patches on the sleeve that he is some kind of baseball star."

"My suspicion is confirmed when the pair stops at a milk bottle booth—one of those joints where, for fifty cents, you get to throw three baseballs at three phony milk bottles. Knock 'em all down and you win a fairly fine prize, in this case a big cuddly teddy bear that the light of my life has set her heart on."

"In no time the local sports fans have gathered to cheer their hero as his state championship arm hurls about five bucks' worth of baseballs at those bottles. Sometimes he tips over one, sometimes he knocks down two, but he never busts out all three. About the fiftieth throw, he makes an awful noise and grabs his arm in pain."

" 'Oh joy!' I think. 'Failure is his!' "

"The pitchman jumps right in and starts trying to convince somebody else to try to win that teddy bear for the little lady, but the injured Bubba-Romeo is growling them off like a pawn-shop dog."

"More stunned by beauty than scared by beast, I step up and toss a half buck at the operator. I never played any school ball but somehow I <u>know</u> I can't fail."

" 'This is for you,' I say to the girl. She smiles—which helps me summon my strength to fire the first ball. 'Boom!' go the bottles. The top one flies ten feet through the air. The other two don't so much as flutter."

"Her dark eyes shining, I rifle the second ball at the bottles. The right one pops up in the air and lands smack on the left bottle which teeters—but doesn't fall. The crowd starts to cheer me on. I turn in the direction of a squeeze on my arm. It's her!"

"Nothing can stop me now. I grip the third ball and bite my lip. The ball makes a 'whoooosh' as it tears through the air, smashing dead-center into the last bottle which tips back to about a 45 degree angle, hangs there for an eternity, then stands back up straight. I can't believe my eyes."

"I stand there frozen in surprise for a moment and when I turn, the light of my life is already walking away with the letter jacket. She gives me a little look over her shoulder that seems to say: 'Too bad, it might have been.' "

"My sleep that night is pretty poor and it isn't helped any when, about five in the morning, I am tossed out of my flea circus/mattress by an awful shaking. It's not the fleas doing the rumba, but one of those terrifying California earthquakes—knocking cheap velvet pictures off the wall, water pitchers off the nightstands, and every can of groceries in town off the shelves and onto the floor."

"Well, I ain't gonna hang around trying to make money from people who really are down and out so the daylight finds me pointed toward greener pastures."

"Heading out, I pass the Mole Bros. Carny and if town is bad, this is worse. The ten-in-one tent is lying flatter than a pancake. Strings of electric lights are strewn across the ground. The ferris wheel is on its side and most of the trailers are piled on top of each other at the bottom of a hole in the ground that wasn't there the day before. All the roustabouts are trying to get an old elephant up off his side and back on his feet."

"And in the whole place the only thing left standing are those three milk bottles."

"It's a lead-pipe cinch!"

CARNY HOT SPOTS

Carny games can be a lot of fun. The honest games, however, are a lot more fun than the dishonest ones.

If you're one of the innocents in the world who believes the carnival is a place you can win something for nothing, note that the common term for a sucker—a "mark"—originated in early carny days. When the operators spotted a real live sucker, they marked his back with a piece of chalk, making it clear to every other rip-off artist in the place that here was a fool with money, an honest-to-goodness "mark."

Some Things to Consider

If you are about to play a carny game because you feel you can win a prize (or money) for less than its value, you are about to be suckered out of some hard-earned cash.

If the game operator is friendly and doing his best to help you out, teach you how to play, or offering to cheat a little for you because he dislikes the boss; run away as fast as you can.

If you don't believe me, save cabfare!

Some Things to Enjoy

If, on the other hand, you want to play because it looks like fun—with no consideration of winnings—you're probably in the right spot.

The safest carny games are the ones in which you compete against other players instead of the store. The most familiar games of this type are the Water Pistol Race and the Horse Race.

NOTE: Before you pay to toss Ping-Pong balls at a fish bowl in order to win a goldfish swimming in a plastic bag, ask yourself a couple of questions: "Do I have an aquarium at home to keep my prize in?" and, if not, "Do I really like sushi?"

1. PENNY FALLS

Inflation has changed this to a game of quarters instead of pennies, but the gaff and the high house odds remain the same.

A pile of quarters lies inside a glass box. On the back side of the coins a flat bar slides to and fro. On the front side is a ledge.

The pigeon drops a quarter in a slot, hoping to land it between the sliding bar and the pile. If the quarter lands just right it will be shoved into the stack, hopefully pushing some of the quarters off the ledge and into the coin return chute, which dumps them out next to the pigeon's pocket. If no coins fall, the fine feathered sucker can always slide another quarter in. The only thing the operator has to do is make change for the turkey's bills—all day long.

Birdbrain gets to keep all the quarters that fall off the ledge except for the ones that fall into the house chute. It's a high-percentage game that's bound to clip your monetary wings.

At twenty-five times the original penny stake, the addictive nature of this game can make it more blood-thirsty than you realize. Listen while you play. The guy making change may be whistling the same song that was heard at the Alamo: "No Quarter."

Ah, but back in those delightful days when it was played for pennies, there must have been a much sweeter song for this kind of carnival fun.

"You'll find your fortune falling
all over town
Be sure that your umbrella
is upside down."

—STEVE MARTIN
Pennies From Heaven

2. BASKETBALL TOSS

So you're a long drink of water that everybody calls "Crazy Legs." In high school you played a pretty mean game of basketball, didn't you? I bet you could make lots of free throws.

All those years of practice are gonna pay off at this game. Surely you can make three in a row for a piddlin' greenback dollar.

But did you practice shooting an overinflated ball at an undersized rim that's two feet too close and only 9' 3" high?

Good luck, Stretch.

> "Just a greenback, a greenback dollar bill,
> It's a little piece of paper,
> Coated with chlorophyll."
>
> —RAY CHARLES

3. SPOTTING THE SPOT

This one <u>used</u> to be played on a board with canvas stretched over it. The mark dropped five disks on a larger spot painted on the canvas. If ya completely covered the spot, ya won a prize. It didn't look too tough. The operator could do it every time.

<u>If</u> you got the first three or four disks down perfectly the operator would *str-etch* the canvas and expose a little red beneath your disks.

The canvas gaff is long gone, but is the game now straight?

It's hard to say: Is the circle round? Perfectly round? Are the disks? The only way to win may be to drop the first disk onto an oblong point in the circle.

Why don't you ask the operator if you can use your compass to check the circle and the disks? I'm sure he'll be very cooperative.

4. STRING PULL

A cute-looking babe of an operator holds a thick bundle of strings which run over her head and are attached to a sea of prizes in the back of the booth. Pheasants, rabbits and various dumb rodents pay to choose a string, give it a pull, and whatever is attached to the other end is theirs to tote home.

The operator even demonstrates the game by pulling on one of the strings and raising an expensive prize. But when the small fry play, the prizes attached to the strings they choose are just a bunch of crud.

The gaff is simple. The very few strings attached to anything of value are turned back in the operator's hand and therefore are unavailable to the paying public.

5. NUMBERS GAMES

(Razzle)

These joints are the big bummer of carnival games. Stay away. Don't go near 'em. You'll have more fun sticking your finger in the flame of a candle <u>and</u> you won't get burned as badly.

Here's how it works.

You pay for a "turn" at rolling several balls or throwing several darts to accumulate a "total." The total is applied to a nearby chart which gives a "score" for your total. As you pay for more turns your score adds to your previous scores for a higher and higher total. If your score reaches a certain level, you win <u>big</u>!

"The more turns you pay for, the better your chances of winning," pitches the operator, mouth drooling for want of a cheap cigar.

Certain scores denote added prizes (if you ever get to a winning total) and also mean added cost per roll. Color television sets and stereos are on display as supposed prizes. The operator can afford expensive prizes because he <u>never</u> gives them away.

Sound somewhat confusing? It is. The average take for this kind of game is probably close to a hundred bucks per sucker.

Even if the operator doesn't cheat by miscounting against you or bringing in new rules as you play, you still haven't got a prayer. Your chances are so bad that the operator occasionally miscounts in your <u>favor</u>, just to keep you interested.

Nobody beats one of these joints, ever.

The true house P.C. varies from game to game and operator to operator, but odds on a particular game of this type were once calculated at over 6 million to one!

"If you want a free ride at the carnival, sneak onto the ferris wheel."

—WILD BILL

Photo by John Tenney

"Horse sense is what keeps horses from betting on what people will do."

—DAMON RUNYON

CHAPTER III

SPORTS & THE TRACK

"Turk, you hockey puck! You're not gonna give my money to some two-bit loan shark. Placing bets with a bookie is about as smart as going to a pawnbroker with two balls."

Wagering on sports events is the biggest sport of all. Billions are risked on everything from football polls to pre-season picks of the World Series winner. But almost all of that money is wagered on games that someone else plays. Spectator gambling is something I generally avoid, if for no other reason than gathering firsthand information at the outdoor games causes me to lose my pool-hall pallor. Besides, this book is about games you participate in.

The track is included because you can go to the paddock and look at the horses when you make your pick, because of the tradition that links wise guys to the ponies and because you can always sit in the club and exchange tips, stories and money with lots of interesting characters.

Best of all, these characters are easily roped into the games we talked about in Book One. What you lose on the horses, you can recoup at the bar.

Ya can't go wrong.

SPORT OF KINGS

(who can afford it)

LET'S LOOK AT THE FACTS

A good thoroughbred horse (bred thoroughly) can run at speeds up to 40 mph. In a one-mile race, a horse averaging 39 mph will finish about 60 yards behind a horse doing 40 mph.

Sixty yards: that's about thirty lengths or about 10 cents of every dollar bet staying with the track.

LET'S LOOK AT THE BETS

Win, Place, and Show

Each of these bets represents an individual pool for which the payoff is determined by the total wagered in each pool and the amount wagered on the horses that finish first (win), second (place), and third (show).

If you bet on a horse to win, you collect if your horse finishes first.

If you bet on a horse to place, you collect if the horse finishes first or second.

If you bet on a horse to show, you collect if the horse finishes first, second, or third.

But That's Not All

If you bet on the Daily Double, you collect if the two horses you bet both finish first in their designated races (usually the 1st & 2nd or the 5th & 6th).

If you bet on the Quiniela, you collect if the two horses you bet (in one race) finish first and second—either horse first.

But That's Still Not All

If you bet on the Exacta (or Perfecta), you collect if the two horses you bet (in one race) finish first and second in the order you designated.

If you bet on the Trifecta, you collect if the three horses you select finish first, second, and third in the order you designated.

Even That Is Not All

Since this book was written, several other bets may have been initiated by your local track or bookie.

So be careful; at the track you might lose the cash in your pocket, but to place a telephone bet with a bookie you don't need any cash in your pocket. All you need is a dime—unless you lose.

1. FORMS & FAVORITES

The Daily Racing Form

Race fans are the only religous fanatics whose bible is printed daily. The legions who regularly decipher the maze of stats in the Daily Racing Form know that, as horse bettors, they are competing against a pari-mutuel pool comprised of a large group of bettors. The odds against the average Joe are high, but if you can learn about the horses, the odds against you may be considerably lower because most bettors are completely ignorant about the ponies.

We all know that the jockeys and the horses' recent records are of prime importance, but lots of "won't-be" winners overlook two essentials: the trainer and the surface.

Good trainers have long careers in the paddock. They know a good horse and they know how and when to run it.

As for the surface, well, some horses like it dry and hard and others like it wet. Me, I like to go when it's really hot or pouring rain and watch the weather play heck with the favorites while I back the long money. Even as a kid I liked to play in the mud.

2. SYSTEMS

The Martingale System

The most famous of all betting systems, the Martingale (or double-up method) is sometimes used at the track with the same disastrous results as anywhere it's tried.

Designed for even-money wagers, the Martingale bettor establishes a betting unit, say five bucks, and wagers that amount on the first bet. Every time he loses, he doubles the bet. Once he wins, he returns to the original five-buck wager. He is now in the profit column (on even-money wagers) for five bucks and starts the sequence again.

It's easy to keep track of and guaranteed to cost you every cent you have. In a losing streak, the rapidly escalating bets ($5, $10, $20, $40, $80, $160, $320) quickly put you over the maximum bet allowed or beyond the limits of your own financial backing. At the end of one bad streak, you're broke.

This system is bad anywhere but it's disastrous at the track where the long odds and finicky ways of the ponies may keep you from having a winner for days or weeks.

Just like at the casino, you'll do better trying to ride out your losing streaks with small bets and increasing the bets only when you can afford it. If you get ahead a pre-determined amount, lock that profit in your wallet and don't take it out for nuthin'. You might quit winners for the day.

Locking the Double

Sometimes called "the wheel," locking is a system for beating the Daily Double. The bettor chooses the most likely favorite in one of the races of the Daily Double and places individual bets on that horse in combination with every likely horse in the other race. If your favorite wins, you got an almost sure daily double winner. If both of the winners are short odds, however, you may not win enough to pay for all of the tickets.

But if you like to bet favorites, the Daily Double and the Exacta are both wagers where you might win some real money.

Racing Form Systems

You see a lot of ads for "can't lose" systems and scientific computer calculators. If these gadgets and formulas were so surefire, would their inventors be willing to sell them to you?

There's no sure thing at the track. Take the twenty-five bucks and put it on a good horse that's five to one. Your odds are about the same.

"This is the only place I know where the windows clean people."

—DUFFY DAUGHERTY

---

3. TOUTS

If you really want to have some fun while you're winning and losing (not necessarily in that order), then you've got to find yourself a bona fide racing tout.

A tout is a person who would have you believe that they possess inside information about a race and, for one reason or another, would prefer to sell that information to you rather than bet on it themselves.

While the information is probably not any more reliable than what you can worm out of the racing forms, it's probably not any worse either. The best part is that oftentimes, a story goes with it. And since the art of the tout is in the sale, be sure to find a tout who tells a good tale. At the worst you'll end up an entertained loser.

"Only madmen and drunks bet on horses."

—NICK THE GREEK

4. THE FIX IS OUT

Switching

A favorite ruse of many classic horse stories, horse switching has pretty much been eliminated by the tatooing of registration numbers on the inside of the horses' lips. It's just as well. It seemed like the wise guys' schemes were always foiled by white horses turning into brown ones during freak thunderstorms.

Valium

Doping horses to run faster or slower has also been reduced to almost nil by saliva and urine tests on all winners. Note that the tests are run only on winners, which doesn't eliminate the possibility that a favored horse that finished poorly may have been slowed chemically.

Past-Posting

In the pre-electronic days of sports reporting, the most common system of ripping off suckers was past-posting the horses. The wise guys would delay the race results at the bookie or off-track betting parlour until a confederate could place some cash on a horse that had already won.

Or a con man might convince a sucker that he had instant access to race results which would enable the sucker to place a massive bet (in the con man's gaming hall) on a supposed surefire winner. But something always went wrong for the sucker.

The world has gotten too fast of late and past-posting is now mostly passé.

However, cheats at casinos now employ a form of past-posting at roulette and craps. One guy physically blocks or distracts the dealer while someone else tosses a couple of crumpled one-dollar bills on a number—just after the ball lands on the number. Even in the unlikely event that the dealer sees the late bet being placed, he may elect to pay it rather than cause a ruckus. However, when he unwraps the one-dollar bills he finds hundreds or thousands on the inside.

The casino does not look kindly on this kind of cheater.

"Hold 'em Back, Boys"

About all that's left to rig a race is getting to one or more of the jockeys, who can pull 'em, hold 'em, or even dump 'em. It's hard to notice and harder to prove but it's nothing the average bettor really needs to worry about because the odds against you are already more than enough to send you home via thumb.

But for my money, watching the horses run is even more fun than shooting craps. You put two bucks or two hundred on a smart-looking pony and watch the sweat and mud fly as your cash comes tearing down the stretch neck-and-neck with somebody else's money.

It's something you ain't never gonna forget.

**"Shoot low, boys,
they're riding Shetland ponies."**

—LEWIS GRIZZARD

Photo by John Tenney

"Pick your co-author carefully."

5. RULES FOR NOT LOSING YOUR PANTS

(AT THE TRACK)

1. **ONLY BET CASH.**
   Bet on credit and sooner or later Fourteen-Week Freddie is gonna show up at your door.

2. **BET TO WIN.**
   The track takes a higher cut from place and show pools. Besides, betting to win is more fun!

4. **DON'T BET STRAIGHT FAVORITES.**
   The low payoffs combined with even a few losers will bust you.

5. **DON'T DISCOUNT BEGINNER'S LUCK.**
   I don't know why but the first trip to the track is the most magical. Take advantage of it and win while it's easy. Once you know what you're doing, it's really hard.

CHAPTER IV

THE STREET

"The Suckers have come home to roost."

—ANONYMOUS PIGEON SHEARER

THE MAN WHO BEAT
MONTE CARLO

"Turk, a word of advice to a rookie. You go out on the street with a hundred bucks of gambling cash and the odds on you are gonna be 5 to 4."

"On winning?"

"No, on living."

Here's a little story. It's all about the three-card monte, Mexico's gift to the grifter. You've seen it: a friendly-looking guy with a tattoo on his nose is tossing some cards around on an overturned cardboard box while a crowd of tourists and other morons give him their cash.

The best of the monte tossers, once upon a time, was a man named Carlo. That's right, Monte Carlo. And he'd never been beat. But, of course, he'd never faced the Amazing Homer, amateur magician from Queens, New York.

One day Homer was taking a lunch break from his midtown Gotham job as a ceiling hanger and he chanced upon a crowd gathered around Monte Carlo. Homer had seen some pretty good card men at Tannen's Magic Shop but he'd never seen anything like Carlo.

A board was laid across two boxes and a crowd was watching Carlo toss the pasteboards with his usual graceful ease. A Japanese lady set a thousand yen down on the card on the right, where Homer was sure the queen was.

From the crowd, another hand shot forward and dropped a twenty on the center card.

"One bet at a time," said Carlo as he handed the lady's money back, turned over the cards and took the other man's twenty. The lady had guessed correctly.

In a flash the cards were tossed again with the seemingly identical moves. Homer winced as the lady put her 1000 yen on the card on the right again. Carlo mentally calculated the exchange rate, called out "$67.00," turned the queen over in the middle and took the yen.

You see, Carlo accepted all the incorrect bets. Only the correct ones were refused.

Filled with outrage and admiration, Homer knew that here was a man to be dealt with! And Homer had a dream: to beat the best; to be known as the man who beat Monte Carlo.

That evening he thumbed through his copy of "The Three-Card Monte" by John Scarne. He practiced the underthrow, the overthrow, and the hipe—tossing the top card in his hand so that it looks like the bottom card had been dropped. A good hipe move is the foundation of any monte tosser's game.

The next day Homer found Carlo in his usual spot: on the sidewalk in front of the police station. He slipped through the crowd and noticed that several of the bettors and onlookers had been there yesterday. They were shills, employees of Carlo and the game.

After tossing the cards, Carlo looked over his shoulder to talk to the people behind him. A guy from the crowd leaned in and turned over the winning queen for everyone to see. Then he bent the corner back at a severe angle and replaced it on the board, jerking his hand back just as Carlo turned back.

When Carlo started tossing the cards without noticing the bent corner, the interest level of John Q. Sucker went up quickly, but when Carlo laid them down and the bent-corner queen was there in the middle for all to see, well it was just too much to resist.

Ten previously reluctant hands reached for wallets and purses and the crowd put up about five hundred bucks. Carlo didn't seem concerned about one bet at a time today. He even let one of the bettors turn over the card and, sure enough, it wasn't the queen. Somehow the bent corner had jumped from one card to another.

The crowd had tried to cheat the guy and it had cost them dearly; 24-karat greed had done them in.

At home, Homer practiced the hipe while watching the cards in the mirror. He could almost fool himself. Almost, but not quite. If sleight of hand wasn't gonna cut it, he'd just have to rely on his ability to select the right card and somehow force Carlo to accept the bet.

That's when he dug out his industrial staple gun, the ceil-tile model. It could fire a steel staple two inches into a thick board!

Homer stuck fifty bucks onto the tip of the staple protruding from the gun and practiced a western-style quickdraw. He had a date with the fastest man on the West Side—at high noon.

The sun reflecting off the Chrysler building at his back, he slipped through the crowd unseen. Carlo was stunned when Homer drew his gun and stapled the fifty dollar bill through the face-down queen and deep into the board.

A silence fell for blocks around.

Homer looked at Carlo. Carlo looked at Homer.

"Well folks, looks like we have another winner!" said Carlo.

The receptionist at the hospital emergency room was just doing her job.

"If you got no health insurance, you're gonna have to pay a deposit or you can't be treated. I'm sorry. That's the rules," she squawked.

"Deposit? How much?" said Homer.

"One hundred dollars."

"No problem. Look closely. There's a fifty that I won stapled to the back of my hand and there's another fifty stuck between my hand and the board. Pull out the staples and wash the bills a little and you got your hundred bucks," Homer said proudly.

After all, he'd just beat Monte Carlo.

Photo by Steve Schapiro

1. THREE-CARD MONTE

When you see somebody win some easy money at the monte, keep in mind that it's a shill, an employee of the game. Lots of folks chase the lady but <u>nobody</u> catches her.

If you believe that card tossers allow you to win one to get you hooked, you're already hooked and halfway to the boat.

If you believe that another spectator, who exposes the queen when the tosser isn't looking, is trying to help you, you're beyond help.

And if anybody says they beat the monte, they're either a liar or they're tougher than the five or six guys that comprise a monte gang.

Nobody, I mean <u>NOBODY</u>, beats the monte!

2. SHELL GAME

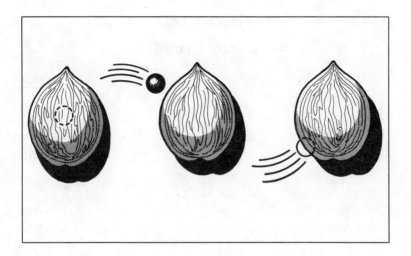

Though not played much on the street anymore, the shell game or thimble-rigging ("Hey diddle-diddle, it's the one in the middle! Which one is it now?") is just another guaranteed hustle.

When the grifter secretly removes the pea, it's called "secretly removing the pea" (or "the steal"). When he puts it back under the shell of his choice, it's called "putting it back under the shell you didn't choose" (or "<u>the load</u>").

With three walnut shells and one pea he can convince you that there's a pea under every shell and one in his hand <u>or</u> that there's no pea at all.

If you like, he'll pull a whole can of peas from under one of those shells.

"Ho, ho, ho!"

—THE JOLLY GREEN GIANT

3. MATCHING COIN SCAM

(Coin Smack)

This could happen to you—anyplace, anytime. Let's say you're waiting to buy a hot dog at the park. Another fellow in the line cracks a joke.

"Say pal, did you hear the one about the missionary in Africa who was about to be eaten by a lion? No? Well, the missionary falls to his knees and begins praying. And right away, the lion kneels and prays too. So the missionary shouts out 'Hallelujah, it's a miracle!' "

"And the lion says: 'You don't understand, I'm saying grace.' "

Laughing, you think how rare it is to meet a likeable stranger. A third fellow in line, a loud fat man, can barely stop laughing. "Say, that's funny! Lemme buy you fellows a hot dog."

"Thanks!" says the joker. "But we couldn't let you do that. I tell you what: let's all match coins for the hot dogs. Odd man pays."

You each flip a coin, call out the result and the joker buys the hot dogs. The fat man cackles how he set you both up and suckered the joker for the wiener

GAMES YOU CAN'T WIN

which fatso is now stuffing into his mouth. He suddenly seems quite repulsive.

"I'll give you clowns a chance to get even," says the fat man. "Let's all match coins, odd man wins both the other two coins."

The fat man steps over to a trash can. The joker comes up with an idea.

"Say, listen. This slob thinks he's a know-it-all. Let's play his game. You call heads and I'll call tails, or vice versa. One of us will always be the winner. We'll pocket the profits and split them behind the bandstand afterwards, okay?"

A half an hour later, the game ends with the joker holding all of Fatso's money and, until the split, all of yours. The whole thing seems too good to be true.

It is. While you're waiting behind the bandstand, the Joker and Fatso are splitting your cash in a nearby bar.

There's one born every minute and you've just been born again.

4. THE LOTTERY

The Dream Game

The lottery is the most played of all street games. Street game, you ask? Yeah, in the twenty-two states that have a lottery, you can play at darn near every corner store in town.

A lottery is a distribution of prizes or cash to winners who are chosen from a large pool of bettors at random. The bettor's chances are determined by: (a) the total number of tickets sold, (b) the number of tickets purchased by the bettor and (c) the number and size of prizes available.

The size of the prize is often determined by the amount of money wagered. However, operating expenses, large advertising budgets and the operator's profit are deducted before prizes are awarded. This doesn't help your odds much.

A percentage of many lotteries is also dedicated to the support of a public institution, i.e. the state school system. This also doesn't help your odds but it is great public relations for the lottery.

In California, for example, 50% of monies taken in is returned to winners and 34% goes to public education. Because the big winners do so well the chances of winning <u>something</u> on each ticket are only 1 in 9.

Many lotteries, in order to provide an immediate thrill to the buyer, have in a sense drawn the winning tickets before they are purchased. The random information on the tickets is obscured by ink that shouldn't be scratched off until the ticket is sold. The gambler's thrill is more immediate but the odds are no better.

So why play? Because the lottery, like Keno, offers an enormous potential payoff for a very small wager. Sure the house may have a 30-percent advantage over you, but we've all read about those payoffs of a million simoleons a year for twenty years. My, my! That's a lot of the long green!

And if you lose, you pay for a few textbooks, something that's hard to knock.

For your dreams, the state thanks you. The schools thank you. And the kids thank you. Thank you.

"A billion here, a billion there—pretty soon it starts to add up to real money."

—SENATOR EVERETT DIRKSEN

CHAPTER V

"SO LONG, SUCKERS!"

Photo by Bob Wallace

"If your cat has kittens in the oven,
you don't call 'em biscuits."

—OLD VERMONTER WISDOM

(Sam Snead once said "You can't cheat a dog," and someone else that was wrong claimed "You can fool most of the people most of the time, but you can't fool Mom." I guess they'd never seen this photo of a spotted dog nursing a leopard kitten.)

Well folks, that's about it. Once I explain to Turk what his true odds are on the street, at the track and in Vegas, he decides to play me on his own ground at his best game: poker.

Personally, I think his odds are much better at the craps table.

"Turk, I hope you've learned something the past few weeks."

"Oh, I have. You gotta keep the windows rolled down when driving on thin ice."

"I mean about winning."

"Winning? Well, Mr. Con Man, let's just play us some poker and find out. I'm from <u>Texas</u> you know."

"Okay, Tex! What's the game?"

"Five-card draw. Deuces, one-eyed jacks and suicide kings wild!"

"Turk, you don't know anything about poker, do you?"

"Sure I do, Harry!"

"You couldn't win a game of poker if you could choose your own cards from the deck. Let's play us a game of Face-Up Poker. You've heard of it, haven't you?"

"Oh, uh . . . yeah! Sure I have."

"We ante up a hundred a piece, I mean I ante a hundred and you ante the hundred I'm paying you for being an idiot in my book. You select any five cards you want. Then I'll select the five I want from the remaining cards."

"Next, you discard and fill your hand from the cards left in the deck. I do likewise and the highest poker hand wins. Whaddya say, Turk O'buddy?"

Well folks, he takes the bait, I mean "bet," and it's a piece of cake—kinda like shooting dead fish in a barrel.

I enjoy the Frenchy champagne his wife is pouring while Turk selects a royal flush: ace, king, queen, jack and ten of spades. I select the same cards in hearts, he declines to discard and so do I.

Since suits have no value in poker (check your "Rules According to Hoyle"), we tie.

Well, there's nothing to do but play again with me selecting cards first. This of course requires another ante and for the first time of the evening some of the sucker's money is in the pot.

I select, not a royal flush, but four tens and a deuce. This puts a worried look on my opponent's face.

"Are deuces wild?"

Reassured that they are not and unable to draw a royal flush because I have all of the tens, Turk selects four aces. Since he is beating me bad, he can't resist saying yes when I offer to double the bet.

I discard all but the ten of spades and draw the nine, jack, queen and king of spades to go with it: a king-high straight flush.

My opponent suddenly discovers that, because the other tens are all in the discard pile, the highest he can draw to is a nine-high straight flush. He is up sucker creek without a paddle or a boat.

Trying not to smile, I pick up all that lovely green money.

The spit knocked out of him, he asks: "Harry, haven't you ever lost?"

I decide to try and cheer him up.

"Sure, I get nailed dead to rights once by an old son of a bachelor with a cane."

"Yeah?" he asks, somewhat encouraged.

As I continue the story his wife pours me some more champagne and begins to rub my weary shoulders. What hospitality!

"This old desert rat bets me five bucks he can bite his right eye."

"And?"

"As soon as I put up my cash, he takes a glassy out of his right eye socket and pops it into his mouth!"

"Wow!"

"Then he offers to bet me double or nothing he can bite the left eye."

"No!"

"Yeah! And I can tell he doesn't have two glass eyes 'cause he can see pretty well. So I toss up another five and he takes out his teeth and bites his left eye!"

"Wow! You can lose," says Turk. "And you're about to bite the big one again. Here's today's newspaper. I bet that you and my wife can't both stand on the top half of the front page without touching each other. Furthermore, I'll bet that you and I can do it! And I'm much bigger than she is."

Well, after springing for the champagne and losing at face-up poker, all he has left is one very lonely dollar bill. It hardly seems worth the trouble but, what the hey, a buck is a buck.

Sure enough, his wife and I can't stand on the paper without touching. In fact, we have to put our hands all over each other just to keep from falling. It's much harder than it first appears.

Half the bet won, Turk opens the front door and sets the paper down in the doorway. Stepping on half, he shuts the door behind him. From outside, we hear his muffled voice.

"Okay, I'm on the paper. You stand on that side."

I am sipping champagne when she turns the lock. Shortly, there comes a light tap from outside the door.

Knock, knock.

"Hey! You owe me a dollar!"

Knock, knock. "Hey! I said . . ."

Photo by John Tenney

Some Words of Wisdom

(Burning Your Sheepskin)

We conclude our course with some practical advice on telling a sheep from a wolf, and on how to go about choosing the best role for yourself.

If you've enjoyed the book and the games within, keep in mind that some of the gambits listed in this book are only good to the extent that your intended victim has not read the book . . . and we intend to sell a <u>lot</u> of copies of this book.

But if you've got a good grasp of what we've covered and you can apply a little personal creativity to your games, we can almost guarantee that you won't end up with an ear full of apple cider. Hopefully you'll be quick enough to only get wet behind your ears.

If you haven't enjoyed the book and you also haven't learned anything, dig out your sales receipt, write the publisher, and they'll tell you what to do with it.

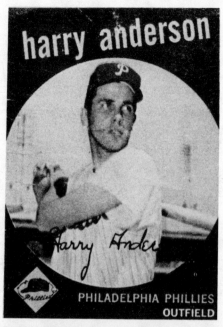

harry anderson

PHILADELPHIA PHILLIES
OUTFIELD

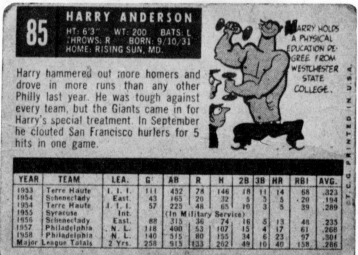

85 HARRY ANDERSON
HT: 6'3" WT: 200 BATS: L
THROWS: R BORN: 9/10/31
HOME: RISING SUN, MD.

Harry hammered out more homers and drove in more runs than any other Philly last year. He was tough against every team, but the Giants came in for Harry's special treatment. In September he clouted San Francisco hurlers for 5 hits in one game.

HARRY HOLDS A PHYSICAL EDUCATION DEGREE FROM WESTCHESTER STATE COLLEGE.

YEAR	TEAM	LEA.	G	AB	R	H	2B	3B	HR	RBI	AVG.
1953	Terre Haute	I. I. I.	111	452	78	146	18	11	14	68	.323
1954	Schenectady	East.	43	165	20	32	5	5	5	20	.194
1954	Terre Haute	I. I. I.	57	225	48	65	16	3	5	39	.289
1955	Syracuse	Int.	(In Military Service)								
1956	Schenectady	East.	88	315	36	74	16	5	13	48	.235
1957	Philadelphia	N. L.	118	400	53	107	15	4	17	61	.268
1958	Philadelphia	N. L.	140	515	80	155	34	6	23	97	.301
Major League Totals		2 Yrs.	258	915	133	262	49	10	40	158	.286

**Don't get ripped off by just any
Harry Anderson . . .**

HARRY THE HAT SEZ

BETCHA CAN'T BOTH STAND ON THE FRONT PAGE

WITHOUT TOUCHING EACH OTHER

I THOUGHT WE COULD DO IT!!

IT'S EASY IF YOU PUT THE PAPER...

UNDER A DOOR!

REMEMBER, HARRY SEZ: DON'T GET MAD, GET EVEN!

'86 HARRY ANDERSON

HT: 6'4" WT: 180 DEALS & TOSSES DICE: L
BORN: 10/14/52 NEWPORT, R.I.

Harry laid off the easy marks last year and concentrated on the big boys: Vegas, Atlantic City & NBC. The good news: his take was way up. The bad news: it's all taxable income.

HARRY'S MAJOR AND MINOR LEAGUE TAKES

YEAR	LEAGUE	MARK	SCORE	METHOD
1957	Bush	Donnie	$1.17	Double-Headed Coin
1972	Street	R.M. Nixon	$200	Shell Game
1979	Minor	Cheers	SAG Scale	Wool Over Eyes
1983	Major	NBC	6 Seasons	Judge

. . . insist on the original!

Photo by Richard W. Bann

"You may already be a loser."

—FROM A LETTER RECEIVED
BY RODNEY DANGERFIELD

1. FINDING YOUR MARK

Now that you've learned some new angles to your gaming, you'll no doubt be thinking about the perfect kind of moron to receive the costly benefits of your wise touch.

Sure, the world is full of both dumb guys and wise guys but most people tend to fall somewhere in the middle. So for Pete's sake, don't go looking for a geek in a *sheer sucker* coat with a pipe and a plastic pencil holder in his breast pocket.

Deep down inside, everyone is a sucker. If dumb guys are a breeze, then smart guys are just a stiff wind. Think about it. The more a wise guy thinks he knows about larcenous doings, the less he'll think a rookie offering a simple wager could ever take him off.

Turk Pipkin is a class kind of sucker. He's easy because he dreams of winning, yet doesn't know how to make his dreams come true. As an inept hustler, the only things that prevent him from receiving black eyes, chipped teeth, and broken bones are his 6' 7" stature and general good nature.

He has the only character trait a con-victim needs: a bit of larceny. What gets the rubes in trouble is that hankering to win something for nothing, even if it's just pride.

Let's make it simple. Just find someone who doesn't know that, in a two-man competition, all you gotta do is finish next to last.

**"It's unlucky to be behind
at the end of the game."**

—DUFFY DAUGHERTY

Photo by Steve Schapiro

2. PLAYING THE PART

Confidence man. Drop the crooked connotations that have been attached to that name and you end up with a good description of a winner: confidence man.

Confidence is an easy concept. You take people into yours and make them forget about their own.

So now you're ready to go out and take the first tentative steps toward confidence manhood. For starters, don't con yourself into believing that clothes really make the con man. Sure, you can go out and buy yourself a nice fedora. I'll even recommend a brand: Borsalino.

You might even want to invest in some nice silk suspenders, a sterling silver hip flask, and some sleeve garters. But don't wear 'em when you're trying to dig up a sucker.

Think about it a minute. Do you want to <u>look</u> like a con man or do you want to <u>win</u> like one?

There's an old story about a guy who takes an elephant to audition for a big theatrical agent. The elephant launches into a fine Al Jolson impersonation, slides into a Judy Garland number, and closes as Baryshnikov—spinning, turning, and leaping twenty feet through the air, landing in full splits!

The agent says: "What's the kid's name? Seymour? Okay. Seymour, come 'ere. Lemme tell you something. I been in this business thirty years and if there's anything I've learned, it's . . . you gotta be yourself."

You may be more ready for the role of part-time huckster than you think. Haven't you run a few little cons in the course of your life? Remember when you faked being sick to stay home from school? How about overstating your qualifications for a job? Or on a loan application? Pulled any recent fast ones on your sweetheart, spouse, or both?

Put that natural training to work in cooperation with your new gaming knowledge and the cash is just naturally gonna flow in your direction.

If all this talk of the exchange of cash bothers your strong sense of morals, remember that, if nothing else, these games provide something to do in a bar other than drink yourself into a stupor.

Besides, an occasional good-hearted swindle is good for you. Onlookers will think you are clever and may assume that you are a notorious kind of person. This is not only fun, it also makes them more likely to cash your non-rubber checks.

Speaking of hot checks, nowhere in this book have I talked about professional crime or petty larceny, but please keep in mind that staying off both of those avenues is strictly up to the reader. I can no more assume responsibility for your legal well-being in these bets and games than I can guarantee the balance of your checkbook. So make sure the numbers add up on the positive side of the line and never, <u>ever</u> bet the kids' college fund.

It's equally important and up to you to insure that game wagers are at a monetary level that your mark can also identify as fun. Don't get your nose broken over a two-headed coin. Just learn when you can win and when you should go home early.

Play the wrong games and you can't win. Play the right games and you just can't lose.

**"You play the black,
and the red comes up."**

3. BIBLIOGRAPHY

Helpful information for this book came from numerous sources, the most important of which, listed below, will prove interesting further reading.

Chafetz, Henry. *Play the Devil*. New York: Clarkson N. Potter, Inc., 1960.

Evans, Mel and Gibson, Walter. *What Are The Odds?* New York: Western Publishing Co. 1972.

Gibson, Walter. *Bunco Book*. Secaucus, New Jersey: Citadel Press, 1964.

McQuaid, Clement, ed. *Gamblers Digest*. Northfield, Illinois: Digest Books, 1971.

Ortiz, Darwin. *Gambling Scams*. New York: Dodd, Mead & Co., 1984.

Ortiz, Darwin. *On Casino Gambling*. New York: Dodd, Mead & Co., 1986.

Potter, Stephen. *The Theory and Practice of Gamesmanship*. New York: Henry Holt and Co., 1931.

Stowers, Carlton. *The Unsinkable Titanic Thompson*. Burnet, Texas: Eakin Press, 1982.

Sullivan, Patrick B. *Bets You Can't Lose.* Los Angeles, California: Price/Stern/Sloan Publishers, Inc., 1979.

Trost, Nick. *Proposition Bets.* Trik-Kard Specialties, 1976.

Trost, Nick. *Expert Gambling Tricks.* Trik-Kard Specialties, 1975.

Thackrey, Ted Jr. *Gambling Secrets of Nick the Greek.* New York: Rand McNally & Co., 1968.

Thompson, Hunter S. *Fear and Loathing in Las Vegas.* New York: Warner Books, 1971.

Wykes, Alan. *Gambling.* Garden City, New York: Doubleday & Co., 1964.